Jesus Spoke In Tongues

James E. Jackson

WESTBOW°
PRESS
A DIVISION OF THOMAS NELSON
& ZONDERVAN

WestBow Press books may be ordered through booksellers or by contacting:

WestBow Press
A Division of Thomas Nelson & Zondervan
1663 Liberty Drive
Bloomington, IN 47403
www.westbowpress.com
1 (866) 928-1240

ISBN: 978-1-4908-6101-2 (sc)
ISBN: 978-1-4908-6103-6 (hc)
ISBN: 978-1-4908-6102-9 (e)

Library of Congress Control Number: 2014921556

Printed in the United States of America.

WestBow Press rev. date: 12/18/2014

Contents

Foreword

The simplistic and repetitious style of this book makes the revelation of God's Word clear and easy to understand. By utilizing the Bible as its ultimate source of authority, this book will prove that Jesus spoke in "other tongues." It shall also prove from Scriptures that all "born again" believers (followers) of the Lord Jesus Christ are commanded by God to follow Jesus into this experience (Eph. 5:19). The ability to speak in other tongues is not a gift that believers should seek to obtain, simply as an end in itself. Believers should always seek to have a deeper relationship with God the Father. They should not simply seek after an experience. The ability to speak in other tongues is instantaneously acquired when a believer receives the baptism of the Holy Ghost. The baptism of the Holy Ghost and speaking in tongues are gifts that are given by God. These gifts helped to give the early Church its supernatural power ("dunamis"). In the Gospel of Matthew, Jesus commanded his disciples to go and teach all nations to "observe all things whatsoever I have commanded you..." (Matt. 28:20a). Throughout this study, the life of Jesus is illustrated, as the example for believers to follow.

Specifically, what is the meaning of the two terms, "baptism of the Holy Ghost" and "speaking in tongues?" To be "baptized in the Holy Ghost" means that a Christian believer receives a greater measure of the Holy Spirit, after salvation. In addition, this greater measure (infilling) of the Holy Spirit also endows the Spirit-filled believer with the ability to speak in "other tongues." "Speaking in tongues" or "tongues" is the supernatural ability given by God to believers, at the time they are filled (baptized) with the Holy Ghost, to speak in a language (tongue) or languages (tongues) that are unknown to the speakers, for the speakers' spiritual empowerment and private worship.

Several terms are used interchangeably, throughout this book. The terms "Holy Spirit" and "Holy Ghost" are used interchangeably. These terms are synonymous. The terms "filled with the Holy Ghost," "filled with the Holy Spirit," "baptized in the Holy Spirit," "baptized in the Holy Ghost," "filled with the Spirit" and "Spirit-filled" are also used interchangeably. These terms are also synonymous.

This study will show that Jesus was baptized in the Holy Ghost and spoke in tongues (Matt. 3:16; Jn. 11:33). Mary, the mother of Jesus, was baptized in the Holy Ghost and spoke in tongues (Acts 1:14, 2:4). The Apostle Paul was baptized in the Holy Ghost and spoke in tongues (Acts 9:17; 1 Cor. 14:18). The Disciples were baptized in the Holy Ghost and spoke in tongues (Acts 2:4). In addition, other believers in the early Church were baptized in the Holy Ghost and spoke in tongues (Acts 10:44, 46). In this book, you will learn that the gift of the Holy Ghost and the gift of tongues are just as available to present day believers, as they were available to believers in the early Church.

Paul said, "Be ye followers of me, even as I also am of Christ" (1 Cor. 11:1). Paul was definitely following Jesus' example, when Paul received the baptism of the Holy Ghost and spoke in tongues. Paul stated, "I thank my God, I speak with tongues more than ye all" (1 Cor. 14:18). The importance of receiving the baptism of the Holy Spirit and speaking in other tongues were some of the basic teachings of the early Church. Let us obediently return to the teachings of the Lord Jesus Christ and his Apostles, who all received the baptism of the Holy Spirit and spoke in tongues.

CHAPTER 1

Trust the Scriptures

This book will present biblical proof that Jesus spoke in other tongues. The validity of Christianity rests on this fact. The credibility of God rests on this fact. In addition, the integrity of the Word of God rests on this fact. If Jesus did not speak in tongues, God is a liar, Christianity is a farce, and the Word of God is a lie.

Jesus assuredly spoke in other tongues, because the Bible shows that speaking in tongues is the one consistent evidence that New Testament believers demonstrated, after they were filled with the Holy Ghost (Acts 2:4; Acts 10:44-46; Acts 9:17; 1 Cor. 14:18). God could not require the disciples to speak in tongues, but not require Jesus to speak in tongues. God would be unjust to require the disciples to do something that He did not require Jesus to do. Moreover, if God is unjust, God would be a liar, Christianity would be a farce, the Word of God would be a lie, and our faith in the Lord Jesus Christ would be in vain!

Fortunately, thanks be to God, we know that God is not a liar, Christianity is not a farce, the Word of God is not a lie, and our faith in the Lord Jesus Christ is not in vain! The Bible provides ample evidence that Jesus spoke in other tongues.

The True Foundation

The key event that provides biblical evidence that Jesus spoke in other tongues is the fact that Jesus was baptized in the Holy Ghost. Jesus received the Holy Ghost. All four Gospels record this particular event.

Matthew 3:16
16 And Jesus, when he was baptized, went up straightway out of the water: and, lo, the heavens were opened unto him, and he saw the Spirit of God descending like a dove, and lighting upon him:

Mark 1:10
10 And straightway coming up out of the water, he saw the heavens opened, and the Spirit like a dove descending upon him:

Luke 3:22
22 And the Holy Ghost descended in a bodily shape like a dove upon him, and a voice came from heaven, which said, Thou art my beloved Son; in thee I am well pleased.

John 1:33
33 And I knew him not: but he that sent me to baptize with water, the same said unto me, Upon whom thou shalt see the Spirit descending, and remaining on him, the same is he which baptizeth with the Holy Ghost.

All other biblical evidence that proves Jesus spoke in other tongues is dependent upon the one fact, that Jesus was baptized in the Holy Ghost. This is true because a believer receives the ability to speak in other tongues, only after he or she is baptized in the Holy Spirit. The Book of Acts is replete with examples of this sequence of events.

Acts 2:4

4 And **they were all filled with the Holy Ghost**, and **began to speak with other tongues**, as the Spirit gave them utterance.

Acts 10:44-46

44 While Peter yet spake these words, **the Holy Ghost fell on all of them** which heard the word.

45 And they of the circumcision which believed were astonished, as many as came with Peter, because that on the Gentiles also was poured out the gift of the Holy Ghost.

46 **For they heard them speak with tongues**, and magnify God. Then answered Peter,

Acts 19:6

6 And when Paul had laid his hands upon them, **the Holy Ghost came on them** and **they spake with tongues** and prophesied.

Acts 9:17

17 And Ananias went his way, and entered into the house; and putting his hands on him said, Brother Saul [Paul], the Lord, even Jesus, that appeared unto thee in the way as thou camest, hath sent me, that thou mightest receive thy sight, and **be filled with the Holy Ghost**.

1 Cor. 14:18

18 I [Paul] thank my God, **I** [Paul] **speak with tongues** more than ye all.

These New Testament Scriptures show that those New Testament believers spoke in other tongues, after they were filled with the Holy Spirit. The baptism of the Holy Ghost came first. Speaking with other tongues came afterward. Even Paul (Saul) who was filled with the Holy Ghost in Acts, chapter nine, gives evidence that he spoke in other tongues after he was filled with the Holy Spirit. He states in First Corinthians, chapter fourteen, "I thank my God, I speak with tongues more than ye all" (1Cor. 14:18).

Not only did the Apostle Paul understand his personal need to be filled with the Holy Ghost and to speak with tongues, Paul taught other believers about the necessity of receiving these two experiences. Acts, chapter nineteen, illustrates how Paul once informed believers about the necessity of receiving these gifts.

Acts 19:1-6

1 And it came to pass, that, while Apollos was at Corinth, Paul having passed through the upper coasts came to Ephesus: and finding certain disciples,

2 **He said unto them, Have ye received the Holy Ghost since ye believed?** And they said unto him, We have not so much as heard whether there be any Holy Ghost.

3 And he said unto them, Unto what then were ye baptized? And they said, Unto John's baptism.

4 Then said Paul, John verily baptized with the baptism of repentance, saying unto the people, that they should believe on him which should come after him, that is, on Christ Jesus.

5 When they heard this, they were baptized in the name of the Lord Jesus.

6 And when Paul had laid his hands upon them, the Holy Ghost came on them; and they spake with tongues, and prophesied.

The necessity of receiving the baptism of the Holy Spirit was not a special miracle that only happened to a few people in the early Church. Unfortunately, today that is what some churches teach. They teach about the importance of receiving water baptism, but omit teaching about the importance of receiving the baptism of the Holy Spirit. However, the baptism of the Holy Ghost was a fundamental doctrine of the early church and was preached and taught throughout its assemblies (Heb. 6:1-2).

Samaritans Spoke in Tongues

Three years after the day of Pentecost, the Samaritans were also filled with the Holy Ghost and spoke with other tongues.[1] The baptism of the Holy Ghost was not simply for the Jews. Luke records the event.

Acts 8:14-18

14 Now when the apostles which were at Jerusalem heard that Samaria had received the word of God, they sent unto them Peter and John:

15 Who when they were come down, prayed for them, that they might receive the Holy Ghost:

16 (For as yet he was fallen upon none of them: only they were baptized in the name of the Lord Jesus.)

17 Then laid they their hands on them, and they received the Holy Ghost.

18 And when Simon saw that through laying on of the apostles' hands the Holy Ghost was given, he offered them money,

Notice that Luke, the writer of Acts, does not record that the Samaritans spoke in other tongues when they "received the Holy Ghost." Luke only records that those particular Samaritans received the Holy Ghost. How then do we know that those Samaritans spoke in tongues after they received the Holy Ghost? We can logically deduce that the Samaritans spoke in other tongues because of what "Simon saw."

Luke records in verse eighteen, "And when **Simon saw** that through laying on of the apostles hands the Holy Ghost was given…"(Acts 8:18). What was it Simon saw that convinced him that the Samaritans had received the Holy Ghost? Luke, in the Book of Acts, records five particular instances where believers were baptized with the Holy Ghost. In four of the five recorded instances in Acts, the Scriptures show that the believers gave evidence that they were filled with the Holy Ghost, by speaking in other tongues (Acts 2:4; Acts 9:17; 1Cor. 14:18; Acts 10:45-46; Acts 19:6).

With this knowledge, we can deduce what it was that Simon saw that convinced him that the Samaritans had received the Holy Ghost. Simon would have undoubtedly seen the same biblical evidence that various believers in Acts demonstrated. They spoke in other tongues when they received the gift of the Holy Ghost. Evidently, Simon saw when hands were laid on the Samaritans to receive the Holy Ghost, they also spoke in other tongues.

Jesus: No Exception

From a superficial perspective, the New Testament seems to give no evidence that Jesus, who is the author and finisher of our faith (Heb. 12:2a), spoke in tongues after he was baptized in the Holy Ghost. The Gospel of Luke records other instances in the New Testament where individuals were filled with the Holy Ghost or had the Holy Ghost come upon them (Lk. 1:13-15, 41, 67; 2:25). Those individuals who received the Holy Spirit or who were anointed with the Holy Spirit before the death and resurrection of Jesus, were living under the dispensation of the Old Covenant. Under the Old Covenant, "the Holy Ghost was not yet given" to the entire Church (Jn. 7:39). Under the Old Covenant, some prophets, some priests, some kings, and some other individuals were anointed with the Holy Ghost or had the Holy Ghost come upon them for purposes of ministry, leadership, administration, artisanship or empowerment.

It is critically important for us to understand that Jesus was baptized in the Holy Ghost and spoke in tongues, because Jesus is the head of the Church (Eph. 5:23). Believers are the body of Christ (1 Cor. 12:27). As the head of the Church, Jesus is the example for the Church to follow. If Jesus did not receive the baptism of the Holy Spirit and speak in other tongues, we, the body of Christ, should not desire these experiences. However, if Jesus, the head of the Church, did truly receive the baptism of the Holy Spirit and did truly speak in other tongues, we, the body of Christ, should follow Jesus and receive these experiences.

In the New Testament, the passion (suffering), death, resurrection, and ascension of Jesus ushered in a New Covenant (Testament). Under the New Covenant, on the day of Pentecost the gift of the Holy Spirit was given to the Church, and thereby made available to the entire body of Christ (Acts 2:1-4). Under the New Covenant, along with the gift of the Holy Ghost, two new spiritual gifts were given to the Church. These two new spiritual gifts were the gift of divers kinds of tongues and the gift of the interpretation of tongues. These two gifts never operated in the Church body prior to the day of Pentecost. Therefore, prior to the day of Pentecost, a few people living under the Old Covenant (e.g., John the Baptist, Elizabeth, and Zacharias) were filled with the Holy Ghost (Lk. 1:15, 41, 67), but they never spoke in tongues, because these two gifts had not been given to the Church at that time.

We have seen several examples of New Covenant believers speaking in tongues, after they were initially filled or baptized with the Holy Ghost. Did Jesus (who was baptized in the Holy Ghost and who ushered in the New Covenant) speak in tongues, or was Jesus the exception?

A minister once illustrated how speaking in tongues accompanies the baptism in the Holy Spirit, under the New Covenant. He said, "Suppose someone gives you a shoe as a gift. If you receive the shoe as a gift, the tongue in the shoe automatically comes with the shoe. If you receive the shoe, you automatically receive the tongue in the shoe, because the tongue is a part of the shoe. Likewise, so it is in receiving the baptism of the Holy Spirit. If you receive the baptism of the Holy Spirit, you automatically receive the ability to speak in other tongues, because the ability to speak in other tongues automatically comes along with the baptism of the Holy Ghost." Therefore, Jesus would have spoken in tongues, because he was baptized in the Holy Ghost, and under the New Covenant the ability to speak in other tongues comes concomitant (together) with the baptism of the Holy Spirit, as a shoe always comes with a tongue.

If a person takes the opposite viewpoint and says that Jesus never spoke in tongues, that person would have to reject the Scriptures, that show the initial observable evidence that believers spoke in other tongues, after they received the baptism in the Holy Spirit. Therefore, to say that Jesus never spoke in other tongues, even though he was baptized in the Holy Ghost (Matt. 3:16; Mk. 1:10; Lk. 3:22; Jn. 1:32), would indicate that Jesus, who is the Word (Jn. 1:14), lacked the abilities that his followers possessed. Because the gifts are of God, Jesus, who is God in the flesh, would have definitely received and operated in all of the gifts of God.

Secondly, if a person says that Jesus did not speak in other tongues, that person is indirectly accusing God of being unjust. It would be wrong for God to require Spirit-baptized believers to speak in other tongues, but not require His Son, Jesus, to do so. If God required other Spirit-filled believers to speak in tongues, but made an exception for His Son, God would be unjust.

Thirdly, if a person says that Jesus did not speak in other tongues, that person is indirectly accusing God of being a respecter of persons. As the head of the Church, Jesus is the example for the Church to follow. Therefore, if God required the body of believers to receive and exercise a spiritual gift, and yet exempt His Son from the necessity of receiving and exercising the same gift, this would show respect of persons. As followers of Jesus, how can we follow him into the experiences of receiving the baptism of the Holy Spirit and speaking in other tongues, if he never operated in these gifts?

So, are the Scriptures in error? Is God unjust? Is God a respecter of persons? Of course, the answer to all three of these questions is, NO! According to Second Timothy, the Scriptures should be our guidebook. We can use the Scriptures for doctrine. We can use the Scriptures for reproof. We can use the Scriptures for correction and for instruction.

2 Timothy 3:16
16 All scripture is given by God, and is profitable for doctrine, for reproof, for correction, for instruction in righteousness:

In addition, according to Psalm nineteen, God is not unjust. God is righteous. He is just and He is pure. David, by the inspiration of the Holy Spirit, states these facts:

Psalm 19:7-9
7 The law of the Lord is perfect, converting the soul: the testimony of the Lord is sure, making wise the simple,
8 The statutes of the Lord are right, rejoicing the heart: the commandment of the Lord is pure, enlightening the eyes.
9 The fear of the Lord is clean, enduring for ever: the judgments of the Lord are true and righteous altogether.

Moreover, according to Romans, chapter two, God is not a respecter of persons, because Paul the Apostle, writes, "For there is no respect of persons with God" (Rom. 2:11). God could not show respect of persons, even to His own Son, neither could Jesus show respect of persons. Jesus could not show respect of persons, even unto his own mother. Neither could Jesus show respect of persons unto any other members of his family. Because the Scriptures are true, and because God is a just God and is no respecter of persons, we can therefore use the Scriptures to show that Jesus received the baptism of the Holy Ghost and spoke in other tongues.

Chapter 2

The Life of Jesus

In order to discover the truth about the life of Jesus, we must go back to the Scriptures, the true Word of God. No matter what we have been taught, if we go back to the Bible, we can separate truth from fiction. Likewise, we can separate truth from partial truth, because partial truth can be just as deceptive as fiction.

We must open our mind to the truth that is found only in God's Word. However, even truth that is filtered through certain denominational teachings or certain church doctrines will become tainted. We must, therefore, lay aside our preconceived ideas, and approach the Word of God with an open mind. We must develop an accurate picture of Jesus' life, in order to follow him in truth—as opposed to following after an error.

The life of Jesus was not ordinary. The earthly life of Jesus started supernaturally and ended supernaturally. The Holy Ghost was paramount in the life of Jesus.

Matthew 1:18-25
18 Now the birth of Jesus Christ was on this wise: When as his mother Mary was espoused to Joseph, before they came together, she was **found with child of the Holy Ghost**.

19 Then Joseph her husband, being a just man, and not willing to make her a publick example was minded to put her away privily.
20 But while he thought on these things, behold the angel of the Lord appeared unto him in a dream, saying, Joseph, thou son of David, fear not to take unto thee Mary thy wife: for **that which is conceived in her is of the Holy Ghost.**
21 And she shall bring forth a son, and thou shalt call his name **JESUS**: for he shall save his people from their sins.
22 Now all this was done, that it might be fulfilled which was spoken of the Lord by the prophet, saying,
23 **Behold, a virgin shall be with child, and shall bring forth a son, and they shall call his name Emmanuel, which being interpreted is, God with us.**
24 Then Joseph being raised from sleep did as the angel of the Lord had bidden him, and took unto him his wife:
25 And knew her not till she had brought forth her firstborn son: **and he called his name JESUS.**

These verses show that Jesus' birth was supernatural. Mary, a virgin and daughter of two human parents, was impregnated by the Holy Ghost. The male baby that was birthed from this union, between God the Holy Ghost and Mary, was named "**JESUS**." Therefore, when Jesus was born, he was both the Son of God and the Son of man.

This does not mean, however, that Jesus had a beginning. Jesus had a birthdate, but he has no birthday. Birthdays connote the beginning of a human being's life, independent from the womb of the mother. Jesus Christ, had a birthdate, i.e., a particular date in which he was birthed into the world. However, Jesus does not have a birthday, i.e., a day that Jesus' existence began. Jesus has always been. He is eternal. He is God. Jesus has been in existence forever. Jesus once prayed to the Father, "... for thou lovedst me before the foundation of the world." (Jn. 17:24c). Jesus' existence did not begin two thousand years ago. John, the Gospel writer, reminds us in his Gospel:

John 1:1
1 In the beginning was the Word, and the Word was with God, and the Word was God.

Notice this verse says that the Word was "with" God, and the Word "was" God. Because God has no beginning, the Word (Jesus) has no beginning, because the Word is God. John, chapter one, verse fourteen tells us that the Word is Jesus.

John 1:14
14 And the Word was made flesh [Jesus], and dwelt among us, (and we beheld his glory, the glory as of the only begotten of the Father,) full of grace and truth.

This verse says that God (the Word) became flesh and blood. God did this by birthing Himself into the world in the form of a human baby, Jesus, the son of Joseph and Mary. Jesus, therefore, had a birthdate (a date that he was birthed into the world as a human being). However, Jesus' existence did not begin on his birth date. Jesus is life and is eternal, he did not begin his life when he was birthed from the womb of Mary (Jn. 5:26).

Can you, the reader, accept these truths, or, are you still filtering the Truth through your denomination's teachings? Faith and belief in our denomination's teachings will not save us. Only Jesus Christ is our Salvation, he is the Word of God made flesh (Rom. 10:9).

The New Birth

The supernatural birth of Jesus sets the pattern whereby you and I can be born into the family of God, as sons and daughters of God. Believers are born into the family of God. We cannot join the family of God by becoming a member of a church congregation.

John 3:3
3 Jesus answered and said unto him, Verily, verily, I say unto thee, Except a man be born again, he cannot see the kingdom of God.

To be "born again" is a supernatural experience that God performs in the heart (spirit) of believers. Salvation ("the new birth") requires that a person receive the person of Jesus Christ as his or her Salvation. In order to receive this supernatural experience, a person needs to do the following four things.

1. Admit that you have broken God's commandments and are in need of God's forgiveness.

Romans 3:23
23 For all have sinned, and come short of the glory of God.

2. Believe that Jesus Christ is God's solution for the penalty of sin.

Romans 4:24-25
24 But for us also, to whom it shall be imputed, if we believe on him that raised up Jesus our Lord from the dead.

25 Who was delivered for our offenses, and was raised again for our justification.

3.   Ask God to forgive you of your sins.

1 John 1:9
9 If we confess our sins, he is faithful and just to forgive us our sins, and to cleanse us from all unrighteousness.

4.   Invite Jesus into your heart (spirit) to be your Lord and your Salvation.

Romans 10:9
9 That if thou shalt confess with thy mouth the Lord Jesus, and shalt believe in thine heart that God hath raised him from the dead, thou shalt be saved.

If a person sincerely performs these four steps, he or she will receive forgiveness of his or her sins, and God will supernaturally cause the human spirit (heart) of the individual to become new. God will literally recreate the person's human spirit (heart) into the image and nature of Christ. In addition, the Holy Spirit will simultaneously takes up residence in the person's newly recreated human spirit (heart). Paul states in Second Corinthians:

2 Corinthians 5:17
17 Therefore if any man be in Christ, he is a new creature: old things are passed away; behold all things are become new.

This happens instantly when a person asks God's forgiveness for his/her sins, and asks Jesus to become his/her Lord and

Savior. The person's physical body and soul (mind, will and emotions) remain the same, but the person's human spirit (heart) becomes recreated. The person becomes a new spiritual person in Christ Jesus. The individual believer must work to conform his or her soul into the image of Christ (Phil. 2:5, 2:13; Rom. 12:2; Mt. 5:44).

Born of the Spirit

The Bible teaches us that all human beings are a combination of three parts – spirit, soul and body. We are spirit beings, we have a soul, and we live in a body. The human spirit and soul of a human being never die. The physical body of a person will eventually die, and after physical death God will judge the human spirit (Heb. 9:27).

1 Thessalonians 5:25
25 And the very God of peace sanctify you wholly, and I pray God your whole **spirit** and **soul** and **body** be preserved blameless unto the coming of our Lord Jesus Christ.

Hebrews 4:12
12 For the Word of God is quick, and powerful, and sharper than any two-edged sword, piercing even to the dividing asunder of **soul** and **spirit**, and of the **joints and marrow** [body], and is a discerner of the thoughts and intents of the heart.

In these two verses, the Word identifies the three parts of our human makeup. Because Jesus was fully human (Phil. 2:6), even though he was simultaneously fully God (Phil. 2:7), Jesus had the same makeup as you and I (spirit, soul and body). We are spirit beings that are clothed in flesh, blood and bone bodies, and we all have a soul (mind, will and emotions).

1. We are spirit beings. God is a Spirit. Humankind was originally created in the image of God. Jesus also has a spirit.

Genesis 2:27
27 So God created **man** in his own **image**, in the image of God created he him; male and female created he them.

John 4:24
24 **God** is a **Spirit**: and they that worship him must worship him in spirit and in truth.

Luke 23:46
46 And when **Jesus** had cried with a loud voice, he said, Father, into thy hands I commend my **spirit**: and having said thus, he gave up the ghost [spirit].

2. We have a flesh, blood and bone body. Jesus also had a flesh, blood and bone body.*

Hebrews 2:14
14 Forasmuch then as the **children** are partakers of **flesh** and **blood**, **he also himself likewise took part of the same**; that through death he might destroy him that had the power of death, that is, the devil;

*Today Jesus has a flesh and bone body, minus his blood (Lk. 24:39). After his resurrection, Jesus took his blood to heaven as payment for mankind's redemption (Heb. 9:11-12).

John 6:53-55

53 Then **Jesus** said unto them, Verily, verily, I say unto you, Except ye eat the **flesh** of the Son of man, and drink his **blood**, ye have no life in you.

54 Whoso eateth my **flesh**, and drinketh my **blood**, hath eternal life, and I will raise him up at the last day.

55 For my **flesh** is meat indeed, and my **blood** is drink indeed.

    3.   We have a soul. Jesus also has a soul.

Mark 12:30

30 And thou shalt love the Lord thy God with all thy heart, and with all thy **soul**, and with all thy mind, and with all thy strength: this is the first commandment.

Matthew 26:38

38 Then said he [Jesus] unto them, My **soul** is exceedingly sorrowful, even unto death: tarry ye here, and watch with me.

We, like Jesus, are spirit beings, with flesh, blood and bone bodies. In addition, like Jesus, we have a soul, which is made up of our mind, our will, and our emotions.[2] In the "new birth" experience, believers are born of the Spirit. Jesus was the first person born of the Spirit (Lk. 1:35; Jn. 3:3-9). The eternal, preexistent Jesus manifested his human (flesh, blood and bone) life on earth as a fertilized embryo, when the Holy Ghost impregnated the egg in Mary's womb. In the new birth, at the exact moment God recreates the human spirit, God the Holy Ghost, also comes and dwells in the newly recreated, righteous human spirit. Believers then have the Holy Spirit in a measure residing inside their human spirit. Our human spirit lives within our flesh, blood and bone body. Paul states, "Know ye not that ye are the temple of God, and that **the Spirit of God dwelleth in you**?" (1 Cor. 3:16). He further states in Second Corinthians, chapter six:

2 Corinthians 6:16
16 And what agreement hath the temple of God with idols? for ye are the temple of the living God; as God hath said, **I will dwell in them**, and walk in them; and I will be their God, and they shall be my people.

God the Holy Ghost dwelt in Jesus, the human being, from the time of Jesus' earthly conception. Jesus was fully God, and fully human. However, even though Jesus was born of the Spirit, he did not become filled or baptized in the Spirit until he was approximately thirty years of age (Lk. 3:22-23). As the Holy Ghost indwelt Jesus, so does the Holy Spirit indwell, in a measure, all born again believers. Moreover, when a born again believer receives the baptism in the Holy Spirit, that individual receives an additional measure of the Holy Spirit. This increase in the measure of the Holy Spirit is in addition to the measure of the Holy Spirit that already resides in the born again believer's recreated human spirit.

When Jesus was baptized in the Spirit, he also received a greater measure of the Holy Spirit, in addition to the measure of the Spirit that he already possessed. However, when Jesus received the baptism of the Spirit, the additional measure of the Holy Spirit that Jesus received was without measure. Followers of Jesus receive the Holy Spirit from God in a measure.

John 3:34

34 For he whom God hath sent speaketh the words of God: for God giveth not the Spirit by measure unto him [Jesus].

Saved From Hell

The "rebirth" of our human spirit reconciles us to God through Jesus Christ. The sin of Adam caused everybody born after Adam to inherit Adam's sin nature. In other words, everyone that is born on the earth is born a sinner, with an inherent sin nature. Hell is God's punishment for sin. In order to avoid going to hell (Matt. 25:41), sinners must receive Jesus as their Salvation, that is, they must become "born again."

John 3:3-7

3 Jesus answered and said unto him, Verily, verily, I say unto thee, Except a man be born again, he cannot see the kingdom of God.

4 Nicodemus saith unto him, How can a man be born when he is old? Can he enter the second time into his mother's womb, and be born?

5 Jesus answered, Verily, verily, I say unto thee, Except a man be born of water and of the Spirit, he cannot enter into the kingdom of God.

6 That which is born of the flesh is flesh; and that which is born of the Spirit is spirit.

7 Marvel not that I said unto thee, Ye must be born again.

Any human being can be "born again." A person must earnestly invite Jesus Christ into his or her heart to be his or her Lord and Salvation. It is important to note that salvation is not only an act of God, salvation is also a Person, the Lord Jesus Christ. Jesus means "SALVATION." Many people agreeably receive the act of salvation, i.e., the act of Jesus dying on the cross for their sins, but they reject receiving the person of Jesus Christ as their SALVATION. In other words, some people readily accept the sacrificial act of Jesus dying for their sins. They do this because they want to avoid going to hell, and personally pay the price for their sins. However, some of these people do not want to form a loving relationship with the Lord Jesus Christ, the one who died for their sins. Jesus died to save them, yet they only want to appropriate the act of God's forgiveness for their sins. They want to receive forgiveness, but they do not want to receive Jesus as their Lord and Master. They want the gift of salvation, but they reject the Giver of Salvation. They reject Jesus. Did you receive the act of Jesus' death on the cross as your salvation, or did you receive the Person of Jesus Christ as your SALVATION? Salvation is a Person. His name is Jesus.

It is true that becoming "born again" saves us from hell, but several other changes take place in the life of every "born again" Christian. 1. The inherently sinful, human spirit is made new and righteous (2 Cor. 5:17). 2. God the Holy Ghost comes and resides in the new (recreated) human spirit (heart) (Col. 1:27). 3. God becomes the Father of each new convert (Christian) (Matt. 6:9). 4. Heaven becomes the promised, future, new home of the Christian (Jn. 14:2-3). 5. The Christian receives spiritual eternal life (Jn. 3:16). 6. The Bible becomes the standard rulebook by which the Christian is to live (Matt. 4:4). 7. The spiritual citizenship of the Christian changes from the kingdom of darkness, to the kingdom of light (Col. 1:13). 8. The Christian becomes a son of God (Jn. 1:12). 9. The Christian becomes an heir of God and a joint-heir with Christ (Rom. 8:17). 10. Satan becomes the Christian's new adversary (1 Pet. 5:8). 11. The Christian becomes eligible to receive the baptism of the Holy Spirit (Matt. 3:11; Jn. 7:37-39; Gal. 3:14).

War in Heaven

Why did Jesus speak in tongues, and why do we need to speak in tongues? One essential reason why we need to speak in tongues is because we, as well as Jesus, have a spiritual adversary. We are all involved in a spiritual conflict (war) that began in heaven before Adam and Eve were created and placed in Eden.

Isaiah 14:12-15
12 How art thou fallen from heaven, O Lucifer, son of the morning! How art thou cut down to the ground, which didst weaken the nations!
13 For thou hast said in thine heart, I will ascend into heaven, I will exalt my throne above the stars of God: I will sit also upon the mount of the congregation, in the sides of the north.
14 I will ascend above the heights of the clouds, I will be like the most High.
15 Yet thou shalt be brought down to hell, to the sides of the pit.

Luke 10:18
18 And he [Jesus] said unto them, I beheld Satan as lighting fall from heaven.

Revelation 12:7-9
7 And there was war in heaven: Michael and his angels fought against the dragon; and the dragon fought and his angels,

8 And prevailed not; neither was their place found any more in heaven.

9 And the great dragon was cast out, that old serpent, called the Devil, and Satan, which deceiveth the whole world: he was cast out into the earth, and his angels were cast out with him.

The instant any person becomes "born again," that person automatically becomes embroiled in a spiritual war: the kingdom of light, against the kingdom of darkness; God and his children, against Satan and His children; God and his armies (hosts), against Satan and His armies (hosts).

God is a Spirit. Satan is a spirit. Angels are spirits. Demons are spirits. Satan's forces of darkness are arrayed against Christians. Satan's tactics are to steal, kill and destroy (Jn. 10:10). He also attempts to seduce Christians back into a life of sin, so that he can again set up strongholds of sin in their lives. Satan's goal is to cause people to reject Christ and to follow him (2 Cor. 4:4-6). Paul writes:

Ephesians 6:11-12

11 Put on the whole armour of God, that ye may be able to stand against the wiles of the devil.

12 For we wrestle not against flesh and blood, but against principalities, against powers, against the rulers of the darkness of this world, against spiritual wickedness in high places.

Paul warns us about our spiritual enemies. He tells us that our real enemies are not flesh and blood, human beings. Our real enemies are the unseen wicked forces, "principalities, powers, rulers of the darkness of this world, spiritual wickedness in high places" (Eph. 6:12). These are demons and evil spirits, whose assignment is to advance the kingdom of Satan and to ensnare the lives of humankind.

Satan wants to keep all of humanity enslaved to sin. Therefore, we must stand strong against the schemes of the Devil. How can we accomplish such a feat? We must "be strong in the Lord, and in the power of his might" (Eph. 6:10b). Again, how do we accomplish this? We must do exactly what Jesus did. Jesus prayed (spoke) in tongues in order to keep himself "strong in the Lord and in the power of his might."

Remember, Jesus was God in the flesh. He laid aside his absolute power and glory, and fully became a human being (Phil. 2:6-7). The fact that Jesus was fully God and fully human, but lived life on earth without his infinite powers and glory, is a new revelation to many Christians. Yet this fact is true. As a man, without the power of God, Jesus was powerless to perform a single miracle or heal a single sickness. In fact, for the first thirty years of Jesus' earthly life, Jesus never performed a single miracle (Lk. 3:23-24). John records the first miracle that Jesus performed. Jesus performed his first miracle at a wedding in Cana of Galilee. At that time, Jesus was about thirty years old.

John 2:10-11

10 And saith unto him, Every man at the beginning doth set forth good wine; and when men have well drunk, then that which is worse: but thou hast kept the good wine until now.

11 This **beginning of miracles** did Jesus in Cana of Galilee, and manifested forth his glory; and his disciples believed on him.

In the first thirty years of Jesus' life, surely he saw sick people that needed healing, but Jesus did not heal a single sick person.

Devoid of his infinite "power and glory," Jesus, as a human being, did not have the power to heal. In addition, surely in the first thirty years of his life, Jesus saw blind people that needed sight, but Jesus did not give sight to a single blind person.[3] Again, this was because, devoid of his infinite "power and glory," as a man, Jesus did not have the power to give sight to the blind.

At age thirty, what happened in Jesus' life that caused him to receive God's supernatural anointing? The answer is, at age thirty, Jesus Christ was baptized (filled) with the Holy Ghost. The Gospels record this event.

John 1:32-34
32 And John bare record, saying, I saw the Spirit descending from heaven like a dove, and it abode upon him.
33 And I knew him not: but he that sent me to baptize with water, the same said unto me, Upon whom thou shalt see the Spirit descending, and remaining on him, the same is he which baptizeth with the Holy Ghost.
34 And I saw, and bare record that this is the Son of God.

Luke 3:21-23
21 Now when all the people were baptized, it came to pass, that Jesus also being baptized, and praying, the heaven was opened.
22 And the Holy Ghost descended in a bodily shape like a dove upon him, and a voice came from heaven which said, thou art my beloved son, in thee I am well pleased.
23 And Jesus himself began to be about **thirty years of age**, being (as was supposed) the son of Joseph, which was the son of Heli.

Baptism in the Holy Ghost

Jesus was baptized in water, but he was also baptized in the Holy Ghost. Various terms are used today to refer to the baptism in the Holy Ghost. The "baptism in the Holy Ghost" is sometimes referred to as: "the baptism in the Holy Spirit," "the baptism of the Holy Spirit," "the baptism of the Holy Ghost," "baptized in the Holy Spirit," "baptized in the Holy Ghost," "Holy Ghost baptized," "Spirit-baptized," and "Spirit-baptism." Additionally, the baptism in the Holy Ghost is also referred to as: "Spirit-filled," "filled with the Spirit," "filled with the Holy Spirit," "filled with the Holy Ghost," "baptism of the Spirit," "infilling of the Spirit," "infilling of the Holy Spirit," and "infilling of the Holy Ghost."

It is important to note, however, that the baptism in the Holy Spirit is separate and distinct from the salvation experience ("born of the Spirit"). Jesus, who was born of the Spirit, was not baptized with the Holy Ghost until he was about thirty years of age (Lk. 3:22-23). This was a time span of about thirty years between the two experiences.

Specifically, what is "the baptism in the Holy Spirit?" The baptism in the Holy Spirit is the experience that an individual receives after salvation, wherein God endows (fills) the "saved" individual with a greater measure of the Holy Spirit, for communion with God, for spiritual edification, and for power (anointing). In short, the baptism in the Holy Spirit is an act of God, whereby God imparts a greater measure of the Holy Spirit into the recreated human spirit ("heart") of a "born again" believer.

The baptism of the Holy Spirit can be received immediately after the salvation experience (Acts 10:43-47), or any time after the salvation experience (Acts 19: 1-6). Under the New Covenant, the exact moment a believer receives the baptism of the Holy Ghost, the believer also receives the supernatural ability to speak in other tongues (Acts 2:1-4). Jesus called the baptism in the Holy Spirit, being "endued with **power** from on high." The word "power" in this verse is a translation of the Greek word "dunamis" in the Greek manuscript. According to "The New Strong's Exhaustive Concordance of the Bible," the word "dunamis" means, "power, ability, strength."[4] This additional power, ability and strength (dunamis) of God was imparted into Jesus' spirit, when he was baptized in the Holy Ghost, around the age of thirty.

Two Separate Acts

As previously stated, "born of the Spirit" ("new birth") and "baptized in the Holy Ghost" ("Spirit baptism") are two distinct and separate experiences. In both of these experiences, "new birth" and "Spirit baptism," a measure of the Holy Spirit is imparted into the believer's human spirit. In the salvation experience ("new birth"), a measure of the Holy Spirit comes and resides in the believer's newly recreated, human spirit. When an individual believes in Jesus Christ and receives salvation by faith, that individual is delivered from the judgment of God and is placed into a right relationship with God (Rom. 10:9-10). In the baptism of the Holy Spirit experience, the believer receives an additional measure of the Holy Spirit, in addition to the measure of the Holy Spirit that he or she received at salvation. This greater measure of the Holy Spirit is what believers need in order to better relate spiritually to God and to do ministry through the power of the Spirit (Jn. 4:24).

Today many denominations preach and teach only about the importance of the salvation experience and the water baptism experience. Also, many of these denominations and churches erroneously teach and preach that a believer receives all of the Holy Spirit that he or she needs when he or she is "born again" ("saved"). The number one goal of these churches is to get people "saved" and get people ready for God's judgment after death. I thank God for the salvation experience and for the ministry of these churches. At least, they are getting people "saved." However, Jesus' number one goal is to get people saved and baptized in the Holy Ghost. His goal is not only to get people ready to die in the by and by, his goal is to also get people ready to live a victorious life in Christ in the here and now. Saved people are called to follow Jesus and receive the baptism of the Holy Spirit.

Today many Christians believe that a person is filled with the Holy Spirit, when he or she receives salvation. Regrettably, this is not true. I reiterate, salvation and the baptism in the Holy Spirit are two distinct experiences. Some charismatic authors have shown that Jesus uses the examples of water in a well and water in rivers to illustrate the two separate experiences.

John 4:10, 14
10 Jesus answered and said unto her, if thou kneweth the gift of God, and who it is that saith to thee, Give me to drink, thou wouldest have asked him, and he would have given thee living water.
14 But whosoever drinketh of the water that I shall give him shall never thirst; but the water that I shall give him shall be in him a **well of water** springing up into **everlasting life**.

John 7:37-39
37 In the last day, that great day of the feast, Jesus, stood and cried, saying, If any man thirst, let him come unto me, and drink. 38 He that believeth on me, as the scripture hath said, out of his belly shall flow **rivers of living water**.
39 (**But this spake he of the Spirit**, which they that believe on him should receive: for the Holy Ghost was not yet given, because that Jesus was not yet glorified.)

The Jews called running water and water issuing forth out of the ground, "living water." Jesus used this imagery of water springing up from an artesian well to illustrate the "new birth" experience to the Samaritan woman at the well. Individuals that ask God's forgiveness for their sins and ask Jesus Christ to be their Lord and Savior, instantly receive God's forgiveness and are "born again" through the Spirit. Jesus calls salvation, "a well of water springing up into everlasting life" (Jn. 4:14).

In chapter seven of John's Gospel, Jesus taught that salvation is not all that God requires of us. In addition to salvation, Jesus taught that believers need to be "filled (baptized) with the Holy Ghost." Jesus uses the imagery of flowing rivers to illustrate the baptism of the Holy Spirit (Jn. 7:38). The baptism in the Holy Spirit is an experience that God wants all "born again" believers to receive, in addition to salvation. Salvation is to have eternal life and the baptism of the Holy Spirit is to have life more abundantly (Jn. 10:10b).

John 7:38
38 He that believeth on me, as the scriptures hath said, out of his belly shall flow **rivers of living water**.

Figuratively, Jesus referred to the new birth as "a well of water." In contrast, Jesus referred to the baptism of the Holy Spirit as "rivers of living water" (Jn. 7:38). The amount of water in rivers is greater than the amount of water that is in a well. Believers are commanded in the Scriptures to receive a greater amount of the Spirit by receiving the baptism of the Holy Spirit, which Jesus also calls "the promise of my Father" (Lk. 24:49). In Acts, Jesus refers to the baptism in the Holy Ghost as "the promise of the Father" (Acts 1:4-5). Peter refers to Spirit baptism as "the gift of the Holy Ghost" (Acts 2:38), and "the promise" (Acts 2:39). In Galatians, Paul refers to the baptism in the Holy Ghost as "the promise of the Spirit" (Gal. 3:14). The baptism in the Holy Ghost is what the disciples received in the Upper Room on the day of Pentecost, when the Holy Ghost was given to the Church (Acts 2:4).

God did not give the Holy Ghost to the Church on the day of Pentecost, and later take Him away. (In the Scriptures, both God and Jesus are attributed with sending the Holy Ghost.) The same Holy Ghost that baptized the disciples is still as present, available and ready to baptize believers today, as He was on the day of Pentecost. Peter proclaimed:

Acts 2:39
39 For the promise is unto you, and to your children, and to all that are afar off, even as many as the Lord our God shall call.

The baptism of the Holy Spirit endued Jesus, the God-man, with supernatural ability and anointing. The supernatural anointing in Jesus allowed God to work His will on earth, through the ministry of a human being, Jesus Christ. It is unlawful for God to come to earth and perform His absolute will by using His unrestrained absolute powers. This would be illegal, because God has given humanity the authority to rule and reign on the earth for a specific time period (Gen. 1:26-28). From the time of Adam, until humanity's "lease" on the earth expires, humanity is the only beings that have God's authority to rule and reign on the earth.

However, Satan usurped humanity's authority to rule on the earth when Adam sinned in the Garden (Gen. 3:60). Satan is now the "god of this world" (2 Cor. 4:4). Satan's kingdom now rules over unregenerate ("lost") humanity. Satan's kingdom is the kingdom of darkness. Until humanity's lease on the earth expires, Satan will continue to usurp human beings' legal right to rule and reign on the earth. Consequently, because God gave legal dominion on the earth solely to mankind, God birthed Himself into the world in the form of a human baby, Jesus Christ, in order to legally take back from Satan, mankind's authority to rule on the earth. God became a man in order to regain the rights that man (humanity) lost, because of the Fall. God could not legally use His absolute powers to rule and reign on the earth, because He had given humanity the authority to rule through Him on the earth.

By becoming a sinless man (the Lord Jesus Christ) and sacrificing Himself for the sins of mankind, God could regain humanity's dominion on the earth. By baptizing Jesus in the Holy Ghost, God could legally work His will on the earth through the man, Jesus Christ (Jn. 5:30). Jesus needed the empowerment of the Holy Ghost (God working through him), to do the work of God on the earth.

The baptism of the Holy Ghost also enabled Jesus to be led by the Holy Spirit. Otherwise, Jesus would have been limited to the parameters of his rational mind (Matt. 4:1). As the head of the Church, Jesus, our example, shows us that we, the body of Christ, are called to be baptized in the Holy Spirit (Acts 2:38-39). God wants to work His will on the earth by using Spirit-baptized believers, who are endued with His supernatural anointing and ability.

Mark 16:17-18
17 And these signs shall follow them that believe, in my name shall they cast out devils; they shall speak with new tongues;
18 They shall take up serpents; and if they drink any deadly thing, it shall not hurt them; they shall lay hands on the sick, and they shall recover.

God gave the Holy Spirit without measure to Jesus (Jn.3:34). Yet, Jesus ministered on earth as a human being ("Son of man"), anointed by God to do the will of God, his Father (Acts 10:38). This is a new concept to many modern day Christians. The Amplified Bible states clearly that Jesus was both God and a human being.

Philippians 2:6-7 (The Amplified Bible)
6 Who, although being essentially one with God and in the form of God [possessing the fullness of the attributes which make God God], did not think this equality with God was a thing to be eagerly grasped or retained;
7 But stripped Himself [of all privileges and rightful dignity] so as to assume the guise of a servant (slave), in that He became like men and was born a human being.

In order to do the works of God, Jesus needed the endowment of the Spirit from God, which is the baptism in the Holy Spirit.

If Jesus needed the baptism of the Holy Spirit to do the works of God, can we, as natural human beings, successfully do the works that God is calling us to do, without the Spirit's baptism? The answer is, NO!

Jesus was God incarnate (in human form). Jesus said, "I and my Father are one" (Jn. 10:30). If Jesus is God (and we know that he is) and he needed to be baptized in the Holy Spirit, we too most certainly need to be baptized in the Holy Ghost.

Two Signs from Heaven

When Jesus was baptized with the Holy Ghost, God demonstrated the occurrence visibly. God sent the Holy Spirit from heaven in the visible form of a dove, which alighted upon Jesus. This demonstration was observed by John, and confirmed for him that Jesus was the one to come, who baptizes in the Holy Ghost (Jn. 1:33). After Jesus received the infilling of the Holy Ghost, God voiced His delight in His Son by saying, "This is my beloved Son, in whom I am well pleased" (Matt. 3:17).

God's pleasure in Jesus also included God's pleasure with Jesus' actions. What action did Jesus accomplish prior to God voicing His pleasure? Immediately prior to God voicing His pleasure in Jesus, Jesus received the baptism of the Holy Ghost. Was God pleased when Jesus received the baptism in the Holy Spirit? The answer is, YES, God was pleased.

There are two obvious reasons why we can definitely conclude that God was pleased when Jesus received the baptism in the Holy Ghost. First, we know that Jesus always did the will of his Father. Jesus states this fact in John, chapter six.

John 6:38

38 For I came down from heaven, not to do mine own will, but the will of him that sent me.

Second, we know that Jesus always did the things that pleased his heavenly Father. Without exception, everything that Jesus did pleased his heavenly Father. In the Gospel of John, Jesus declares:

John 8:29

29 And he [the Father] that sent me [Jesus] is with me: the Father hath not left me [Jesus] alone; for I [Jesus] do always those things that please him.

Because the Scriptures prove that Jesus came to do the will of his Father, and that he always did the things that pleased his Father, we can conclude: 1. When Jesus was baptized with the Holy Ghost, he was doing the will of his Father. 2. When Jesus was baptized with the Holy Ghost, he was doing what pleased his Father.

Because Jesus was doing the will of his Father when he received the baptism of the Holy Ghost, are we in the Church today doing the will of the Father, when we do not receive the infilling of the Holy Ghost? Furthermore, because Jesus always did what pleased his Father, he was doing what pleased the Father when he received the baptism of the Holy Ghost. Are we in the Church today doing what is pleasing to God, when we do not receive the infilling of the Holy Ghost? You decide.

Approximately three and a half years after God demonstrated the Holy Ghost baptism of Jesus, by sending the visible form of a dove from heaven, Jesus demonstrated the Holy Ghost baptism of believers by sending the sound of a mighty rushing wind from heaven, and the visible appearance of tongues of fire.

Acts 2:1-4
1 And when the day of Pentecost was fully come, they were all with one accord in one place.
2 And suddenly there came a sound from heaven as of a rushing mighty wind, and it filled all the house where they were sitting.
3 And there appeared unto them cloven tongues like as of fire, and it sat upon each of them.
4 And they were all filled with the Holy Ghost, and began to speak with other tongues, as the Spirit gave them utterance.

John the Baptist had proclaimed that Jesus would baptize with the Holy Ghost and with fire (Matt. 3:11). After Jesus's death, resurrection, and ascension into heaven, Jesus fulfilled the promise of his Father by sending the Holy Ghost to the Church on the day of Pentecost (Acts 2:1-4). Jesus demonstrated this event by sending an audible and a visible sign. Believers in the Upper Room heard the sound of a rushing mighty wind. The sound of the rushing mighty wind signified the coming of the Holy Ghost.

Believers in the Upper Room also saw flames of fire in the shape of cloven (split) tongues. They saw a cloven tongue of fire sitting upon each of the believers. The term "tongues" in the New Testament primarily means "languages," e.g., in First Corinthians, chapter thirteen. Paul wrote, "Though I speak with the tongues of men and of angels, and have not charity, I am become as sounding brass, or a tinkling cymbal" (1 Cor. 13:1). Paul uses the term "tongues" in this verse, which means "languages." Similarly, in Acts, chapter two, the term "tongues" means "languages." After the believers received the baptism in the Holy Ghost, they began to speak in other tongues (languages), as the Holy Spirit gave them the ability.

Bible Evidence

From Pentecost onward, the Holy Ghost has been present in the world to indwell believers and to baptize them in the Holy Ghost. Jesus used the visible sign of tongues of fire resting upon each believer, to signify the visual presence of the Holy Ghost. Each flame of fire was shaped in the form of a tongue, which divided at the end. The Scriptures calls these tongues "cloven tongues", which means they divided at the end, such as the hooves of a cow or goat are divided, and are called cloven footed. The cloven tongues signified dual or multiple languages. However, the visible signs of cloven tongues of fire resting upon the believers were not evidence that these believers had received the baptism in the Holy Ghost. The main evidence that the Bible gives as proof that believers had received the baptism of the Holy Ghost is the believers spoke in other tongues or languages.

Acts 2:4
4 And they were all filled with the Holy Ghost, and **began to speak with other tongues**, as the Spirit gave them utterance.

Acts 10:44-46
44 While Peter yet spake these words, the Holy Ghost fell on all them which heard the word.

45 And they of the circumcision which believed were astonished, as many as came with Peter, because that on the Gentiles also was poured out the gift of the Holy Ghost.

46 For **they heard them speak with tongues**, and magnify God. Then answered Peter,

Acts 19:6

6 And when Paul had laid his hands upon them, the Holy Ghost came on them; and **they spake with tongues**, and prophesied.

Paul seems to be an exception to this norm. Luke, the writer of Acts, does not record that Paul spoke in tongues when he received the baptism of the Holy Ghost. However, Luke's omission of this occurrence is not proof that Paul did not speak in tongues when he received the baptism of the Holy Ghost. Possibly, Luke was inspired by the Holy Spirit not to include such a detail in his account. Let us examine Luke's account more closely.

Acts 9:17-18

17 And Ananias went his way, and entered into the house; and putting his hand on him said, Brother Saul, [Paul] the Lord, even Jesus, that appeared unto thee in the way as thou camest, hath sent me, that thou mightest receive thy sight, and be filled with the Holy Ghost.

18 And immediately there fell from his eyes as it had been scales: and he received sight forthwith, and rose and was baptized.

Clearly, there is no indication that Paul spoke in tongues after he was initially filled with the Holy Ghost. However, we are told in First Corinthians that Paul could speak in tongues, and did often speak in tongues. He records this fact in First Corinthians, chapter fourteen:

1 Corinthians 14:18
18 I thank my God, I [Paul] speak with tongues more than ye all.

Many people in the Church today are against speaking in tongues. They try to find Scriptures to support their belief. The Apostle Paul, however, commanded the church in Corinth not to forbid believers to speak in tongues. He writes, "Wherefore, brethren, covet to prophesy, and **forbid not to speak with tongues**" (1Cor. 14:39).

Paul was not an exception to the norm. He too spoke in tongues. Therefore, Jesus, who was also baptized in the Holy Ghost, would be an exception to the norm, if he did not also speak in tongues. Again, God would be an unjust God, if He required believers to do something that He did not require Jesus to do. As we shall see, Jesus, indeed, spoke in tongues.

CHAPTER 3

Jesus (God and Man)

Have you ever wondered why it was possible for Jesus to perform so many miracles? Some people might assume that Jesus was able to perform miracles because he was the Son of God. It is true that Jesus was fully God, "for in him dwelleth all the fullness of the Godhead bodily" (Col. 2:9). However, at the same time Jesus was fully God (Son of God), he was also fully a human being (Son of man). Jesus was not God on some occasions and a human being on other occasions. Neither was Jesus half God and half man. Jesus was simultaneously fully God and fully human, throughout his earthly life.

Although he was fully God (Jn. 1:1, 14), he laid aside his inherent attributes of omnipotence (having all power), omniscience (having all knowledge), and omnipresence (having all presence), and became a human being. Jesus was God, Who self-limited Himself and became a finite human being.

So, where did Jesus get his supernatural, miracle-working power? The answer might surprise you. Though Jesus was the Son of God, he never performed a single miracle as the Son of God, neither as the Son of man. It was God the Father, working through Jesus, Who performed the miracles in Jesus' earthly ministry. Jesus stated this fact plainly to Philip, in the Gospel of John, chapter fourteen.

John 14:10
10 Believeth thou not that I am in the Father, and the Father in me? the words that I speak unto you I speak not of myself: but **the Father that dwelleth in me, he doth the works**.

Again, in John, chapter five, John records Jesus' proclamation, that he can do nothing of his own accord. Jesus' actions reflected the will of God. Jesus declared that he is not the one who does the works, but it is God Who does the works through him.

John 5:17, 19, 30
17 But Jesus answered them, My Father worketh hitherto, and I work.
19 Then answered Jesus and said unto them, Verily, verily, I say unto you, The Son can do nothing of himself, but what he seeth the Father do: for what things soever he doeth, these also doeth the Son likewise.
30 I can of mine own self do nothing: as I hear, I judge: and my judgment is just; because I seek not mine own will, but the will of the Father which hath sent me.

We can see from those verses of Scripture that Jesus never performed a single miracle by his own power. It was God working through the anointing in Jesus, that performed every miracle in Jesus' ministry. How was it possible for God the Father to work through Jesus, the Son of man? It was possible for God the Father to work through Jesus, the Son of man, because Jesus was baptized in the Holy Ghost and anointed (empowered) by God to do the works of God. In the Book of Acts, Luke writes:

Acts 10:38
38 How God anointed Jesus of Nazareth with the Holy Ghost and with power: who went about doing good, and healing all that were oppressed of the devil; for God was with him.

God used the empowerment of Jesus' Holy Ghost baptism to work His will on earth through Jesus, a human vessel. Take for example, the electrical appliances in your home. Some appliances require more electricity to operate than some other appliances. The amount of electrical volts needed to operate your computer is less than the number of volts needed to operate your refrigerator. Therefore, the power cord to your computer is smaller than the power cord to your refrigerator. The smaller the electrical wire, the less voltage it can conduct. The larger the electrical wire, the greater the voltage it can conduct. Metaphorically, a Christian is wired to receive and conduct the power of God in a limited capacity. However, after receiving the baptism in the Holy Spirit, that Christian receives "larger wiring" to receive and conduct the power of God on a greater capacity. Metaphorically, have you received larger wiring to receive and conduct the greater power of God? Are you baptized in the Holy Ghost?

Jesus was not birthed on earth simply to show that God could work miracles. The miracles verified that Jesus was who he said he was, the Son of God, who came to do the will of his Father. God became Jesus, who lived an exemplary life and ultimately gave His life as a sacrifice for the sins of the world. John writes in his first epistle:

1 John 2:2 (The Amplified Bible)
2 And He – that same Jesus Himself – is the propitiation (the atoning sacrifice) for our sins, and not for ours alone but also for [the sins of] the whole world.

When John the Baptist beheld Jesus, he proclaimed, "Behold the Lamb of God, which taketh away the sin of the world" (Jn. 1:29b). Jesus came to die as a sinless man for the sins of the world. In addition, Jesus also came to live on earth as a human being, who received the baptism of the Holy Ghost. God wants every believer in the body of Christ to receive the baptism of the Holy Ghost. He wants to work His will on earth through Spirit-filled Christians. Paul uses the analogy of a body and its head to illustrate our Christian relationship with Jesus. Jesus (the head of the body) and his body (the Church) are one body. A body does not work contrary to its head. A body works in agreement with the will of its head. Therefore, Christians, as the body of Christ, should not work contrary to the works of Jesus, who is the head of the body. Neither should Christians, as the body of Christ, work contrary to the will of Jesus. Paul confirms in First Corinthians and in Ephesians, that Jesus is the head of the Church, and the Church must be subject to its head.

Ephesians 5:23-24
23 For the husband is the head of the wife, even as **Christ is the head of the church**: and he is the savior of the body. 24 Therefore as **the church is subject unto Christ**, so let the wives be to their own husbands in every thing.

1 Corinthians 12:12-14, 27

12 For as the body is one, and hath many members, and all the members of that one body, being many, are one body; so also is Christ.

13 For by one Spirit are we all baptized into one body, whether we be bond or free; and have been made to drink into one Spirit.

14 For the body is not one member, but many.

27 Now **ye are the body of Christ**, and members in particular.

As the body of Christ, we are commissioned by God to continue the ministry of Jesus. God wants to minister through us the same way that He ministered through Jesus, using the power of the Holy Ghost. Jesus ministered through the power and anointing of the Holy Ghost. This power (though in a lesser degree) is promised and available to every believer. Jesus declared to his disciples:

Luke 24:49

49 And, behold, I send the promise of my Father upon you: but tarry ye in the city of Jerusalem, until ye be endued with power from on high.

The earthly ministry of Jesus is not supposed to be a onetime phenomenon, a onetime event that we look back upon and simply proclaim. We are called, as the body of Christ, to carry on the present day ministry of Jesus, by working with God, through the power and the anointing of the Holy Ghost (Matt. 28:19-20). Jesus went back to heaven so that the Holy Ghost could come and dwell within believers, to empower believers with a greater measure of the Spirit of Christ (Jn. 16:7).

Jesus the Man

Many modern day Christians will agree that Jesus is the Son of God. They will also agree that Jesus is a divine being. However, not all believers will agree that Jesus has equality with God. Nevertheless, Jesus is God and he declared his equality with God. Jesus declared, "I and my Father are one" (Jn. 10:30). Jesus is one hundred percent God, just as God the Father is one hundred percent God. Equally important, Jesus is one hundred percent God, just as the Holy Spirit is one hundred percent God. God the Father, God the Son (Jesus) and God the Holy Spirit are all one hundred percent God. The oneness of God the Father, God the Son and God the Holy Spirit is called the "Godhead" (Col. 2:9). They are not three gods. They are three modes of the same God.

Deuteronomy 6:4
4 Hear, O Israel: The Lord our God is one Lord:

Colossians 2:9
9 For in him [Jesus] dwelleth all the fulness of the Godhead bodily.

We can illustrate the oneness of the Godhead by using a glass of water. We can take a glass of water and place it on a dinner table. The water is in the form of a liquid. Next, we can take the same water and place it in the deep freezer for three hours. When we take the water out of the freezer, the water will have frozen solid. Its form has changed. At first, it was a liquid. Now, it has become a solid. Next, place the solid ice from the glass into a saucepan and heat the pan on the stove until the ice melts and the water begins to boil. Continue boiling until all of the water in the saucepan evaporates. The ice will have changed into water, then into steam (a gas). The water changed its form three times. It is the same water (liquid), yet it became ice (solid) and steam (gas). Similarly, God the Father, God the Son and God the Holy Ghost are three modes of the same God, yet they are one God.

Jesus was God without Power

God is unlimited in power. He is omnipotent, omniscient and omnipresent. However, as stated previously, God, though unlimited in power, cannot come into the world and do whatever He desires to do. God has given humanity dominion (rule) over the earth. Therefore, God must work through humankind, in order to accomplish His will on the earth. Genesis, chapter one, shows that God gave "man" (humanity) dominion over the earth.

Genesis 1:26-28
26 And God said, Let us make man in our image, after our likeness: and **let them have dominion** over the fish of the sea, and over the fowl of the air, and over the cattle, and **over all the earth**, and over every living thing that moveth upon the earth.
27 So God created man in his image, in the image of God created he him; male and female created he them.
28 And God bless them, and God said unto them, Be fruitful, and multiply, and **replenish the earth, and subdue it**: and have dominion over the fish of the sea, and over the fowl of the air, and over every living thing that moveth upon the earth.

God gave humanity authority to rule over the earth. This is similar to a present day landlord leasing an apartment to a tenant for a term of one year. If the tenant pays his or her rent and upholds the terms of the lease agreement, the tenant has the authority to live in the apartment for one year. Even though the landlord still owns the apartment, the landlord cannot come over, unlock the apartment, come in and rearrange the furniture. Nor, can the landlord come into the apartment and cook a meal in the kitchen or throw a party in the living room. Though the landlord owns the apartment, the landlord does not have the authority to do these things as long as the apartment is under lease to the tenant. Similarly, though God owns the earth, He has given humanity the legal authority (similar to a lessee) to perform His will on the earth, throughout the duration of mankind's "lease" on the earth.

Unfortunately, humanity chose to disobey God, and to follow Satan (Gen. 3:6-7). Because of mankind's disobedience to God, Satan took over humanity's authority to rule over the earth. Satan became the "god of this world" (2 Cor. 4:3-4), and is ruling over unregenerate ("lost") humanity. In Luke, chapter four, Satan declared to Jesus that he possesses the right to rule over the earth.

Luke 4:5-6
5 And the devil, taking him [Jesus] up into an high mountain **shewed unto him all the kingdoms of the world** in a moment of time.
6 And the devil said unto him [Jesus], All this power will I give thee, and the glory of them: **for that is delivered unto me**; and to whomever I will I give it.

Satan is still presently "the god of this world" and will continue to be so, until God's predetermined timetable for humanity to rule over the earth ends. God's desire is to set humanity free from the dominion of Satan, and from sin and its bondages (spiritual death, sickness, poverty, and demonic influences). Human beings are the only entities who have been given legitimate authority to rule on the earth. God wanted to redeem (buy back) humanity from sin and Satan, but God needed to use a man to redeem humanity. God needed a sacrifice, a sinless man, to pay the price for humanity's redemption. (The use of the term "man" in this discussion is not male chauvinism.) Sin was passed to the human race, not through the woman, Eve, but through the disobedience of the man, Adam (Rom. 5:19). God, therefore, needed a sinless man in order to redeem humanity. However, all humanity is born with Adam's inherent sin nature. Therefore, there were no sinless men (or women) in existence. God, therefore, had to become a sinless man (Jesus) in order to redeem humanity. God birthed Himself into the world (in the mode of sinless Jesus), in order to pay the price for humanity's redemption. Through faith in Jesus' sacrificial death, humanity can receive deliverance from Satan's kingdom of darkness and become a citizen of God's kingdom of light (Col. 1:13-15).

Even though Satan is still the god of this world, Jesus' defeat of Satan at Calvary (Col. 2:11-15) gave Christians authority in the name of Jesus, to exercise dominion over the kingdom of darkness. God requires believers to enforce their dominion and deliverance from Satan's kingdom. This can be compared to the 1945 military defeat of Japan by the United States. Even though the United States defeated Japan in World War II, the U.S. government had to send soldiers into Japan to occupy its territory, in order to ensure that Japan's defeat was enforced.

The U.S. military entered Japan and disarmed Japan's military. The armed U.S. soldiers in Japan were in a foreign territory, yet they had the authority of the U.S. government to occupy and enforce the United States' dominion over Japan. Japan would have otherwise continued to work unrestrained against the United States. Similarly, Jesus defeated and disarmed the kingdom of Satan (Col. 2:15). Jesus made it possible through faith, for believers to be delivered from the kingdom of darkness, and to receive authority and power to enforce their dominion over the spiritual kingdom of darkness (1 Jn. 5:4).

Though defeated and disarmed, Satan and his kingdom still war against God's kingdom. Through killing, stealing and destroying (Jn. 10: 10), Satan still reigns over the fallen world. Satan will continue to reign over the fallen world until the time period of humanity's "lease" to rule the earth expires (Rev. 11:15).

As followers of Jesus Christ, we are soldiers in the army of the Lord. God desires to work through believers, in order to advance His kingdom in the earth. God's kingdom and the kingdom of darkness are both spiritual kingdoms. Jesus said, "Neither shall they say, Lo here! or, lo there! for, behold, the kingdom of God is within you" (Lk. 17:21). The kingdom of God is the will of God being done in the earth. Human strength alone cannot advance the kingdom of God. Believers need God's supernatural empowerment (Holy Ghost baptism) in order to stand strong against the wiles of the enemy and to advance God's will in the earth (Acts 1:8).

John 6:63
63 It is the Spirit that quickeneth; **the flesh profiteth nothing**: the words that I speak unto you, they are spirit, and they are life.

Zechariah 4:6

6 Then he answered and spake unto me, saying, This is the word of the Lord unto Zerubbabel, saying, **Not by might, nor by power, but by my spirit**, saith the Lord of hosts.

Jesus needed a physical body to operate legitimately in this world. Jesus needed a body that was strong and healthy, in order to walk and minister throughout the land of Israel. However, Jesus did not come to establish the kingdom of God through his physical prowess. Physical strength alone cannot establish the kingdom of God. Jesus needed physical strength, but he also needed spiritual strength, in order to combat Satan and his spiritual hosts (Eph. 6:12).

Lifting weights can increase the body strength of a weight trainer, but what can increase the spiritual strength of a believer? The answer is, speaking in tongues can increase the spiritual strength of a believer (1 Cor. 14:4a). Therefore, Jesus needed to be baptized in the Holy Spirit and speak in tongues, in order to keep himself spiritually empowered (charged up).

Previously, we have read in the Scriptures where believers were initially baptized with the Holy Ghost, and gave evidence by speaking in other tongues. We have also seen that Paul spoke in tongues, though the Scriptures do not record that he immediately spoke in tongues after he was initially filled with the Holy Ghost. Moreover, though the Scriptures do not record that Jesus spoke in other tongues when he was initially baptized in the Holy Ghost, we will discover three different occasions in the Scriptures where Jesus spoke in other tongues.

CHAPTER 4

Jesus Prayed in Tongues in the wilderness

After Jesus was baptized with the Holy Ghost, he was led by the Spirit into the wilderness to be tempted by the devil. How did Jesus know to go into the wilderness? Rational sense knowledge did not lead Jesus into the wilderness. Jesus was "led by the Spirit", i.e., he was led by the Holy Ghost into the wilderness.

Luke 4:1-2
1 Jesus being full of the Holy Ghost returned from Jordan, and was **led by the Spirit** into the wilderness.
2 Being forty days tempted of the devil. And in those days he did eat nothing: and when they were ended, he afterward hungered.

We sometimes think that Satan tempted Jesus constantly for forty days. We think that Jesus' total time in the wilderness was occupied constantly fighting off Satan's temptations. However, the Scriptures reveal that the last recorded temptation of Jesus in the wilderness only took a moment of time.

Luke 4:5 (Amplified Bible)
5 Then the devil took him up to a high mountain, and showed Him all the kingdoms of the habitable world **in a moment of time** – in the twinkling of an eye;

Not only do the Scriptures show that the last recorded temptation of Jesus took a short amount of time, the Scriptures also show that Satan was not continually in the presence of Jesus. In fact, the Scriptures show that the devil would temporarily leave Jesus. The Amplified Bible states this fact very clearly.

Luke 4:13 (Amplified Bible)
13 And when the devil had ended every [the complete cycle of] temptation, he left Him – temporarily, that is, stood off from him until another more opportune and favorable time.

Because Jesus was not tempted continuously for forty days, what else was Jesus doing those forty days? Luke, chapter four, verse fourteen gives us insight into what Jesus was doing in the wilderness, other than fasting and being tempted of the devil. The answer is, Jesus was praying in tongues. Luke presents the evidence that Jesus spoke in tongues in the wilderness. Luke records, "And Jesus returned in the power of the Spirit into Galilee" (Luke 4:14a). It is interesting to note that Luke records that Jesus was "full of the Holy Ghost" when he went into the wilderness. Equally important, is the fact that Luke records that Jesus returned from the wilderness "in the power of the Spirit." Jesus came out of the wilderness differently than how he went into the wilderness. Jesus went into the wilderness "full of the Holy Ghost," but returned from the wilderness "in the **power of the Spirit**."

Again, the word "power" used here, is translated from the Greek word "dunamis," from which we get the words "dynamite" and "dynamo." The New Strong's Exhaustive Concordance of the Bible, further defines "dunamis" as, "miraculous power, ability, abundance, meaning, mighty (-ily, -y deed), (worker of miracles), power, strength, violence, mighty (wonderful) work".[5]

Jesus went into the wilderness "full of the Holy Ghost." What made him return "in the **power** of the Spirit?" There seems to be a progression from being "full of the Holy Ghost" to walking "in the **power of the Spirit**." The word "power" used here is the same Greek word used for "power" when Jesus said, "But ye shall receive **power**, after that the Holy Ghost is come upon you".

Acts 1:8
8 But ye shall receive power, after that the Holy Ghost is come upon you: and ye shall be witnesses unto me both in Jerusalem, and in all Judea, and in Samaria, and unto the uttermost part of the earth.

Jesus was stating that believers shall receive miraculous power and strength after they have received the Holy Ghost. He was not stating that believers shall receive physical power and strength. Jesus was referring to believers receiving spiritual power and strength. This power is the same kind of intensified power (dunamis) that Jesus possessed, when he returned from the wilderness.

How was Jesus able to walk in this miraculous spiritual power and strength of God? Was it because he was the Son of God, who naturally had the power to work miracles? The answer is, No, because it has been previously shown from the Scriptures that Jesus gave up his divine power, and became a finite human being, though without sin (Phil. 2:6-8).

The power (dunamis) that Jesus walked in did not come because he was God. The power that Jesus walked in came because of what Jesus did as a human being. Miraculous spiritual power and strength could be manifested through Jesus because he prayed in tongues. Praying in tongues was Jesus' avenue to extraordinary spiritual power.

"He that Speaketh in an Unknown Tongue Edifieth Himself"

Paul states in First Corinthians, chapter fourteen, "He that speaketh in an unknown tongue edifieth himself" (1 Cor. 14:4a). Speaking in tongues "edifieth" the person that does the speaking. The word "edifieth" is translated from the Greek word "oikodomeo." "Oikodomeo," according to Strong's Exhaustive Concordance of the Bible, means, "to be a house-builder, i.e., construct or confirm – (be in) build (-er, -ing, up), edify, embolden".[6]

Speaking in tongues spiritually "builds up" the believer who does the speaking in tongues. "Building up" has the connotation of "charging up," as a battery is charged up.[7] A battery has power when it is charged up. Webster's New World Dictionary defines a battery as, "a connection of cells storing an electrical charge and capable of furnishing a current".[8] A discharged battery is a battery that has little or no remaining stored energy. In order to restore power to a discharged battery, the battery must be "charged up", i.e., "edified" (oikodomeo).

The human spirit of a born again believer can be compared to a battery. The conflicts and trials of daily life can cause the human spirit to discharge its spiritual power, like a battery. Similarly, the human spirit is capable of being charged up spiritually. Speaking in tongues is the electrical charge or flow of the Holy Ghost that supercharges the human spirit. When believers receive the baptism in the Holy Spirit, they also receive the ability to speak in other tongues. Speaking in tongues spiritually builds up (edifies) the human spirit of the believer. Little or no speaking in tongues results in less power (dunamis). More speaking in tongues results in more power (dunamis).

For example, it is much easier to use your car when your car's battery is fully charged. Trying to start a car when the car's battery is weak is problematic. It is even more difficult to play the car's radio, blow the car's horn, burn the car's lights, or run the car's heater when the car's battery is weak. Similarly, it is much easier for God to work through a believer, whose spirit is charged or edified, than for God to work through a believer, whose spirit is spiritually discharged.

Luke says, "And Jesus returned in the power of the Spirit into Galilee." In other words, Jesus was "built up" or "charged up" in the Spirit when he returned from the wilderness. In order for Jesus to return from the wilderness "in the power of the Spirit," he had to have prayed in tongues in the wilderness.

"Building up Yourself on Your Most Holy Faith"

Jude also writes about the spiritual power that comes from speaking in tongues. In his epistle, Jude makes it clear that praying in tongues builds up (edifies) the speaker. Praying in tongues is a form of speaking in tongues. Jude writes in verse twenty, "But ye, beloved, **building up yourselves** on your most holy faith, **praying in the Holy Ghost**." The phrase, "praying in the Holy Ghost" refers to praying in tongues. In addition, Paul, in his first letter to the Corinthians, refers to praying in tongues as, "praying in the Spirit." He states:

1 Corinthians 14:13-15b
13 Wherefore let him that speaketh in an unknown tongue pray that he may interpret.
14 For if I pray in an unknown tongue, my spirit prayeth, but my understanding is unfruitful.
15 What is it then? I will pray with the Spirit, and I will pray with the understanding also.

Here Paul refers to praying in tongues as, "pray with the Spirit." Jude, therefore, is referring to praying in tongues, when he uses the phrase, "praying in the Holy Ghost." In both experiences, the believer is speaking in tongues. Jude, in verse twenty, says that praying in the Holy Ghost (praying in tongues) builds up "yourselves." The term that Jude uses, "building up," is the Greek word, "epoikodemo," from the same word for "edify" (oikodomeo). Both Paul and Jude agree that "praying with the Spirit" (praying in tongues) and "praying in the Holy Ghost (praying in tongues) edify (build up) the speaker spiritually. The Living Bible records Jude, verse twenty, in clearer and simpler language.

Jude 20 (The Living Bible)
20 But you, dear friends, must build up your lives ever more strongly upon the foundation of our holy faith, learning to pray in the power and strength of the Holy Ghost.

Jesus came ministering in power (dunamis). He kept himself "built up" by "learning to pray in the power and strength of the Holy Ghost," i.e., by praying in tongues. Jesus was not simply a preacher of righteousness. His ministry was not simply a ministry of proclamation. His ministry was a ministry of demonstration, power and proclamation. After Jesus' wilderness experience, Jesus came into Galilee preaching the kingdom of God, in Word and in demonstration. He not only preached the kingdom of God, he also demonstrated the power of God's kingdom. These facts are evident throughout the Gospels.

Luke 11:20 (Today's Living Bible)
20 But if I am casting out demons because of power from God, it proves that the kingdom of God has arrived.

Luke 7:22
22 Then Jesus answering said unto them, Go your way, and tell John what things ye have **seen** and **heard**; how that the blind see, the lame walk, the lepers are cleansed, the deaf hear, the dead are raised, to the poor the gospel is preached.

A fully charged battery, allows electricity to flow out through its cells, directly into a car's electrical system. Conversely, a discharged battery needs to be replenished with electricity, before electricity can flow through its cells and into a car's electrical system. Similarly, Jesus needed to keep himself edified (built up) spiritually by praying in tongues, in order for the Holy Ghost to flow through him and into the needs of humanity. Praying in tongues spiritually builds up (edifies) a believer, which makes it possible for the believer to operate and flow more freely in the Spirit. Though Jesus had the Spirit without measure, he still had to keep himself spiritually charge up by praying in tongues. How do you keep yourself spiritually charged up?

The Secret of Jesus' Prayer Life

It is apparent from Scripture that Jesus prayed in tongues, because Jesus' prayer life had a one hundred percent success rate. God fulfilled every petition that Jesus ever asked of Him. Jesus was confident that God would grant every petition that he asked. We know that Jesus prayed with confidence, because of the prayer that he prayed at the tomb of Lazarus.

John 11:41-42
41 Then they took away the stone from the place where the dead was laid. And Jesus lifted up his eyes, and said, Father, I thank thee that thou hast heard me.
42 And I knew that thou hearest me always: but because of the people which stand by I said it, that they may believe that thou hast sent me.

Why was it possible for Jesus to always pray with confidence? Jesus prayed with confidence, because Jesus knew that God always heard him when he prayed. Why did God always hear the prayers that Jesus prayed? It was because Jesus always prayed "according to the will" of God. John clarifies why we need to pray according to the will of God.

1 John 5:14-15
14 And this is the confidence that we have in him, that if we ask anything according to his will, he heareth us,

15 And if we know that he hear us, whatsoever we ask, we know that we have the petitions that we desire of him.

Did God always hear and grant Jesus' petitions because Jesus was the Son of God? Is that why God always gave special attention to Jesus' prayers? The answer is, No, because God would be a respecter of persons, if he respected the prayers of Jesus, over the prayers of others. Fortunately, we know that God is not a respecter of persons, because the Scriptures confirm this fact.

2 Chronicles 19:7

7 Wherefore now let the fear of the Lord be upon you; take heed and do it: for there is no iniquity with the Lord our God, **nor respect of persons**, nor taking of gifts.

Acts 10:34

34 Then Peter opened his mouth, and said, Of a truth I perceive that **God is no respecter of persons**:

We can see from these two Scriptures that God does not show favoritism among people. Therefore, God never showed favoritism to Jesus when he prayed. Jesus had a successful prayer life, because he always prayed the will of God. Jesus was the Logos (Written Word) of God, made flesh (Jn. 1:14). Jesus was also the Rhema (Spoken Word) of God, made flesh (Eph. 6:17). Jesus was the Word of God revealed. Jesus was the revelation of God the Father. Because Jesus was the revelation of the Word of God (both Rhema and Logos), the words that Jesus spoke, which included his prayer life, were a revelation of the will and Word (Logos) of God. Jesus, therefore, only spoke the words of his Father (Jn. 12:49-50). The Gospel of John states, "For there are three that bear record in heaven, the Father, the Word, and the Holy Ghost: and these three are one" (1 Jn. 5:7).

Jesus stated to Philip, "he that hath seen me hath seen the Father (Jn. 14:9c). By making that statement, Jesus was confirming the fact that he is the revelation of the will and Word of God. Jesus states in John, chapter six, "For I came down from heaven, not to do mine own will, but the will of him that sent me" (Jn. 6:38). Additionally, in chapter twelve of the Gospel of John, Jesus states:

John 12:49-50

49 For I have not spoken of myself, but the Father which sent me, he gave me a commandment, what I should say, and what I should speak.

50 And I know his commandment is life everlasting: whatsoever I speak therefore, even as the Father said unto me, so I speak.

Because Jesus was birthed into the world as a human being, he possessed a human will, just as you and I. However, Jesus never exercised his will to do anything that was contrary to the will of God. Even in his prayer life, Jesus prayed the will of his Father. Matthew records Jesus praying the will of his Father, as he prayed in the Garden of Gethsemane.

Matthew 26:39

39 And he went a little farther, and fell on his face, and prayed, saying, O my Father, if it be possible, let this cup pass from me: nevertheless **not as I will, but as thou wilt.**

We can now understand why Jesus always got his prayer petitions answered by God. It was because Jesus always prayed the will of God. Equally important, John states that we, believers, can ask anything according to God's will, and God will also hear us, and grant our petition (1 Jn. 5:14-15).

Interestingly, how did Jesus know the will of God in every situation? Was it because Jesus was the omniscient (all knowing) Son of God? No, because we know that Jesus divested himself of his divine powers, and was born on earth as a normal human being.

Because Jesus was a human being, he was limited in knowledge, and could not know the will of God in every situation. However, when Jesus prayed in tongues, he always prayed the will of God in every situation, because praying in tongues enables Spirit-filled believers to articulate the will of God in prayer (Rom. 8:26-27). The Holy Ghost enabled Jesus to pray the perfect will of God. Just as Paul prayed with the spirit and prayed with the understanding, Jesus also prayed with the spirit, and prayed with the understanding also (1 Cor. 14:15). Both Jesus and Paul prayed in other tongues and both Jesus and Paul prayed in their everyday language. One reason God sent the Holy Ghost was to enable Spirit-baptized believers to pray in tongues (1 Cor. 14:15). John writes:

John 14:16-17 (The Amplified Bible)
16 And I will ask the Father, and He will give you another Comforter (Counselor, **Helper**, Intercessor, Advocate, Strengthener, and Standby) that He may remain with you forever. 17 The Spirit of Truth, Whom the world cannot receive (welcome, take to its heart), because it does not see Him, nor know and recognize Him. But you know and recognize Him, for He lives with you [constantly] and will be in you.

God sent the Holy Ghost to earth to be our Counselor, Helper, Intercessor, Advocate, Strengthener, and Standby. The Holy Ghost, as our Intercessor, helps Spirit-filled believers in their prayer life. Paul states in Romans:

Romans 8:26-27
26 Likewise the Spirit also helpeth our infirmities: for we know not what we should pray for as we ought: but the Spirit itself maketh intercession for us with groanings which cannot be uttered.
27 And he that searcheth the hearts knoweth what is the mind of the Spirit, because he **maketh intercession** for the saints **according to the will of God.**

Paul states that we do not know what we should pray for, as we ought. Therefore, he says the Holy Spirit helps us by making intercession (prays in our behalf) for us, according to the will of God. Unfortunately, many people think that Paul is saying that the Holy Ghost prays for us independently of our involvement. However, this is not true. On earth, the Holy Ghost does not pray for us independently of our involvement. The Holy Ghost was sent to earth to work in and through us, not to work independently from us.

The Holy Ghost does not pray in tongues. It is the Spirit-filled believer that actually does the vocal praying in other tongues (Acts 2:4; 10:46; 19:6; 1 Cor. 14:14-15). The Holy Ghost gives the Spirit-filled believer the ability to articulate the words that the Holy Ghost wants to speak or pray through the believer. However, the Holy Ghost does not articulate or speak in tongues. The believer does the articulating, the speaking, and the praying in tongues.

Because Jesus lived on earth as a human being, he could not have known the will of God in every situation and circumstance. However, the Holy Ghost, Who is God in Spirit, always knows the will and mind of God. As our Intercessor or helper, the Holy Ghost helps us to pray the will of God in tongues. In order to pray the will of God in every situation, Jesus needed to pray in tongues. A believer who prays in tongues always prays the will of God (Rom. 8:27), because praying in tongues always articulates the will of God.

Praying in tongues assures us that we are praying in exact accord with the will of God. John says, whenever we pray according to God's will, God hears us, and we know that we have the petitions that we desired of him (1 Jn. 5:14-15). Jesus could pray with confidence, because he knew that God always heard his petitions and would grant his petitions. How do we know that we are praying the will of God, and that God will hear us and grant our petition? Of course, the answer is, when we pray in tongues, we are praying the will of God.

The prayer life of Jesus was a mystery to his disciples, because Jesus kept his prayer life private. Jesus would withdraw himself from his disciples, and go to an isolated place and pray. Jesus' disciples could attest to the miraculously, effective prayer life of Jesus, yet they did not know how Jesus prayed. Therefore, the disciples implored him, "Lord, teach us to pray" (Lk. 11:1b). At that time, Jesus could not teach his disciples about praying in tongues (in the Spirit), because the Holy Ghost had not yet been given to the Church (Jn. 7:39). Jesus could only teach his disciples to pray according to their natural understanding. He taught them to pray the model prayer that we call "the Lord's Prayer" (Matt. 6:9-13). This short prayer takes less than one minute to pray. Jesus, however, sometimes prayed all night. This kind of praying, praying with the understanding, could not have engaged Jesus for long periods, without becoming repetitious. Furthermore, Jesus clearly warns us against praying repetitious prayers. He states, "But when ye pray, use not vain repetitions, as the heathen do: for they think that they shall be heard for their much speaking" (Matt. 6:7). However, praying in tongues can be engaged in for long periods of time, without becoming repetitious. Jesus did not use "vain repetitions" when he prayed. How did Jesus avoid praying repetitious prayers? Jesus prayed in tongues. We can now understand how Jesus maintained a one hundred percent effective prayer life.

Chapter 5

Jesus Prayed in Tongues
at Lazarus' Grave

"...he groaned in the spirit, and was troubled." (Jn. 11:33d)

This chapter will elaborate upon the fact that Jesus prayed in tongues at the tomb of Lazarus. Let us take an exegetical (interpretive) look at what Jesus really said in verse thirty-three, in the eleventh chapter of John. However, in order to understand what is transpiring in verse thirty-three, it is necessary to read several preceding verses that pertain to the story of Lazarus.

John 11:1-15, 30-33
1 Now a certain man was sick, named Lazarus, of Bethany, the town of Mary and her sister Martha.
2 (It was that Mary which anointed the Lord with ointment, and wiped his feet with her hair, whose brother Lazarus was sick.)
3 Therefore his sister sent unto him, saying, Lord, behold, he whom thou lovest is sick.
4 When Jesus heard that, he said, this sickness is not unto death, but for the glory of God, that the Son of God might be glorified thereby.
5 Now Jesus loved Martha, and her sister, and Lazarus.

6 When he had heard therefore that he was sick, he abode two days still in the same place where he was.

7 Then after that saith he to his disciples, Let us go into Judaea again.

8 His disciples say unto him, Master, the Jews of late sought to stone thee; and goest thou thither again?

9 Jesus answered, Are there not twelve hours in the day? If any man walk in the day, he stumbleth not, because he seeth the light of the World.

10 But if a man walk in the night, he stumbleth, because there is no light in him.

11 These things said he: and after that he saith unto them, Our friend Lazarus sleepeth; but I go, that I may awake him out of sleep.

12 Then said his disciples, Lord, if he sleep, he shall do well.

13 Howbeit Jesus spake of his death: but they thought that he had spoken of taking of rest in sleep.

14 Then said Jesus unto them plainly, Lazarus is dead.

15 And I am glad for your sakes that I was not there, to the intent ye may believe; nevertheless let us go unto him.

30 Now Jesus was not yet come into the town, but was in that place where Martha met him.

31 The Jews then which were with her in the house, and comforted her, when they saw Mary, that she rose up hastily and went out, followed her, saying, She goeth unto the grave to weep there.

32 Then when Mary was come where Jesus was, and saw him, she fell down at his feet, saying unto him, Lord, if thou hadst been here my brother had not died.

33 When Jesus therefore saw her weeping, and the Jews also weeping which came with her, **he groaned in the spirit**, and was troubled.

The phrase "he groaned in the spirit," is often misunderstood by modern readers. Notice the Scripture text does not say that Jesus simply "groaned." The Scripture states that Jesus "groaned in the spirit." The word "groaned" is translated from the Greek word "embrimaomai." According to Strong's Exhaustive Concordance of the Bible, "embrimaomai" means, "(to snort with anger); to have indignation on; to blame; to sigh with chagrin; to sternly enjoin; -- straitly charge; groan; murmur against."[9]

Bible translators have translated "embrimaomai" in several ways. They have translated "embrimaomai" to mean that Jesus "groaned." They have translated it to mean that Jesus "had indignation on." They have translated it to mean that Jesus "sighed with chagrin," etc. Nevertheless, no matter how differently Bible translators translate the word "embrimaomai," most translators agree on the translation of the phrase "in the spirit." Therefore, no matter what translators say "embrimaomai" means, most translators agree that "embrimaomai" was done "in the spirit."

Fortunately, Paul uses the word "groanings" (stenagmos) in his writings. By studying what Paul meant by "groanings," we can better understand what Jesus did when he "groaned in the spirit." Paul's letter will reveal to us what Jesus actually did at the tomb of Lazarus. In Romans, chapter eight, verse twenty-six, Paul writes:

Romans 8:26
26 Likewise the Spirit also helpeth our infirmities: for we know not what we should pray for as we ought: but the Spirit itself maketh intercession for us with **groanings which cannot be uttered**.

"Groaning in the Spirit" is Praying in Tongues

The Greek word "stenagmos" is translated "groanings" in Romans, chapter eight, verse twenty-six. Strong's Exhaustive Concordance of the Bible defines "stenagmos" as, "a sigh: -- groaning."[10] The root word for "stenagmos" is the word "stenazo," which means, "to make in straits; to sigh; murmur; pray inaudibly: -- with grief; groan; grudge; sigh."[11] Notice that "stenazo" means more than "groan" or "sigh." "Stenazo" also means to "pray inaudibly." It is very evident that Paul is talking about prayer in this verse when he says, "the Spirit itself maketh **intercession** [prayer] for us." "Intercession," according to Webster's New Universal Unabridged Dictionary, means "the act of interceding; mediation between conflicting parties with a view to reconciliation; prayer or pleading in behalf of another or others, or sometimes against another."[12] How does the Holy Spirit pray in our behalf? The answer is, through "groanings" (inaudible prayers) which cannot be uttered. "Groanings" are inaudible prayers.

Many people assume that "inaudible" means "not able to be heard." In fact, this is exactly how Webster defines it. According to Webster, "inaudible" means "not audible; that cannot be heard."[13] Therefore, if we think of "groanings" as "inaudible prayer," we will probably think that "groanings" are prayers that cannot be heard. However, the word "inaudible" can also mean that something is heard, but it is not understood. Webster lists these synonyms for the word "inaudible": "low, suppressed, stifled, muffled, still, soundless, silent."[14]

Here is an example of a sound that is inaudible. Have you ever sat near someone who was talking on the telephone? You could intelligibly hear every word the person was saying, who was sitting near you. In addition, you heard every word the person was saying, on the opposite end of the telephone, but you could not intelligibly understand what he or she was saying. The person's voice on the other end of the phone was "inaudible" – you could hear it, but you could not understand it intelligibly.

Coincidentally, if the person on the phone sitting near you asked, "Did you hear my friend talking on the phone?" You could answer, "No, I did not hear your friend" – meaning, that you did not understand what the friend was saying. You only heard the sound of his or her voice. You could also answer, "Yes, I heard your friend talking" – meaning, you heard the sound of the friend's voice, but you did not understand the words that the friend was saying. The friend's words were "inaudible" – that is, they could be heard, but not understood. Luke gives us a Scriptural example that illustrates this occurrence. In retelling Paul's Damascus Road experience, Luke records:

Acts 9:7

7 And the men which journeyed with him stood speechless, **hearing a voice**, but seeing no man.

Notice, Luke records that the men heard a voice. Conversely, in retelling the same story in Acts, chapter twenty-two, Luke records that the men did not hear a voice.

Acts 22:9

9 And they that were with me saw indeed the light, and were afraid; but they **heard not the voice** of him that spake to me.

In Acts, chapter nine, it states that the men heard a voice. In Acts, chapter twenty-two, it states that the men did not hear a voice. This seems like a clear contradiction, until we understand the uniqueness of the word "inaudible." "Inaudible" can mean that something is entirely not picked up by the ear, i.e., something that is not heard. Conversely, "inaudible" can mean that words or sounds are heard, but they are unintelligible. The New Testament: An Expanded Translation gives us a clearer understanding of these two verses.

Acts 9:7 (The New Testament: An Expanded Translation)
7 And the men who were journeying with him stood speechless, hearing indeed the voice as a sound only and not understanding the words, moreover not seeing anyone.

Acts 22:9 (The New Testament: An Expanded Translation)
9 And those with me saw indeed the light but did not hear the voice of the One speaking to me so as to understand the words, but heard it merely as a sound.

In both of the Scripture passages a sound was heard, but the words were not understood. In other words, the words were heard, but they were "inaudible." The words were not heard with enough clarity to understand what was said.

The same is true in reference to "groanings." "Groanings" can be defined as "inaudible prayer." Inaudible here means that the prayer can be heard, but the prayer is unintelligible. Let us read Romans, chapter eight, verse twenty-six again to see what Paul really meant.

Romans 8:26
26 Likewise the Spirit helpeth our infirmities: for we know not what we should pray for as we ought: but the Spirit itself

[Himself] maketh intercession [prayer requests] for us with groanings [inaudible prayers] which cannot be uttered.

These "groanings" or "inaudible prayers" are simply audible prayers that are prayed in unintelligible speech. They are prayers that are audibly prayed by a person or persons through the ability of the Holy Spirit. These "goanings" or prayers are unintelligible because they are prayed in a language that is not understood by the hearer or hearers.

Paul states that these "groanings" (inaudible prayers) "cannot be uttered." "Uttered," according to Strong's Exhaustive Concordance is translated from the Greek word "alaletos," which means: "unutterable, which cannot be uttered."[15]

The phrase, "which cannot be uttered," conveys the meaning: "which cannot be uttered (spoken) in articulate speech;" or "which cannot be spoken in intelligible speech," or "which cannot be spoken with understanding." Therefore, when Paul says, "which cannot be uttered," he is referring to utterance that is not spoken in understandable human speech. It is simply an utterance that is spoken in a language (tongue) that is not understood by the hearer or hearers.

"Groanings" are therefore not sounds, but speech in a language that is unintelligible. The Tyndale New Testament Commentaries on Romans states that, "with groanings which cannot be uttered" can mean, "speaking to God in the Spirit with tongues."[16]

The Holy Ghost Intercedes for Us

Paul states, that the Spirit makes "intercession [prayer requests] for us with groanings [inaudible prayers]." Many people who read this verse think that Paul is saying that the Holy Ghost automatically prays for "us" without our human participation. However, upon further exegesis (interpretation) of this passage we will learn that the work of the Holy Spirit is to work in conjunction with "us" (the body of Christ), not to work independently from us. Jesus illustrates this point when he calls the Holy Spirit, "Comforter." Jesus said in John, chapter fourteen:

John 14:16
16 And I will pray the Father, and he shall give you another Comforter, that he may abide with you forever.

The word "Comforter" is translated from the Greek word "parakletos," which means, "an intercessor, consoler: -- advocate, comforter," according to Strong's Concordance.[17] Kenneth Wuest, in his book, Word Studies in the Greek New Testament, states, "The verb parakaleo refers to the act of calling someone to one's side in order to help one. The noun parakletos refers to the one who is called upon to render aid. It is used in the courts of one who pleads another's cause before a judge, a counsel for the defense, an adovcate. In the widest sense it means "a helper, a succorer, one who aids another."[18]

We can understand from these definitions that the "Comforter" (Holy Ghost) is sent to be our helper, as one alongside of us. The "Comforter" was not sent to do our praying for us, and we simply do nothing. The Holy Spirit (Comforter) intercedes for us in conjunction with our efforts.

How does the Holy Spirit intercede for us in conjunction with our efforts? When a Spirit-filled believer prays in tongues, the Holy Spirit supernaturally gives the believer the ability

71

to articulate the words that are expressed. The Holy Ghost does not pray in tongues. The believer does the praying in tongues. The believer must vocally articulate the words (prayer petitions) that the Holy Spirit wants to intercede through him or her. Therefore, when Paul says, "but the Spirit itself maketh intercession for us," he does not mean that the Holy Ghost independently prays for us. Paul is stating that it is the Holy Spirit that gives the believer the ability to express in tongues, the express will of God for a particular situation. Thus, praying in tongues is the Holy Ghost interceding through us. This type of prayer is "inaudible" or "unutterable," which means that it is spoken in a language (tongue) that is usually unintelligible to human understanding.

"Groaning in the Spirit" is, therefore, the Holy Spirit interceding through us, when we pray in tongues.* This brings us back to our original Scripture. Let's read John, chapter eleven, verse thirty-three again.

John 11:33
33 When Jesus therefore saw her weeping, and the Jews also weeping which came with her, he groaned in the spirit, and was troubled,

*(However, we should note that not all speaking in tongues is praying in tongues. In addition, not all praying in tongues is intercession. There are various forms of tongues, e.g., speaking in tongues (1 Cor. 13:1), praying in tongues (1 Cor. 14:14) and singing in tongues (1 Cor. 14:15). There are also various kinds of prayer in tongues, e.g., prayers of thanksgiving (1 Cor. 14:16-17), prayers of edification (Jude 1:20) and prayers of intercession (Rom. 8:26). Further elucidation of the various diversities of tongues is beyond the scope and intent of this present study.)

Here is the phrase again, "groaned in the spirit." However, from studying what Paul meant, we now know this phrase means, "praying in the Holy Ghost," which is, praying in tongues. Therefore, here in John, chapter eleven, when it says that Jesus groaned in the spirit, it means that he spoke or prayed in tongues. This shows Scriptural evidence that Jesus spoke in tongues. Do you speak in tongues?

CHAPTER 6

Jesus Spoke in Tongues on the Cross

Mark 15:34-35

34 And at the ninth hour Jesus cried with a loud voice, saying, Eloi, Eloi, lama sabachthani? Which is, being interpreted, My God, my God, why hast thou forsaken me?

35 And some of them that stood by, when they heard it said, Behold, he calleth Elias.

This utterance of Jesus from the cross is most controversial. It is controversial because of the theological implications of God's abandonment of Jesus on the cross. It is also controversial because this statement (Mk. 15:34) of Jesus on the cross is in an unknown tongue.

Many biblical scholars state that the language spoken by Jesus in this verse is Aramaic. They state that Aramaic was the language learned by the Jews during their Babylonian captivity. Many believe that Aramaic was the everyday, common language spoken by the Jews.[19]

However, more recently a growing number of noteworthy scholars are rejecting this claim. These scholars state that evidence from the Dead Sea Scrolls and evidence from Scriptures prove that Jesus and the Jews of his time spoke Hebrew, not

Aramaic. Some scholars who support this belief are Dr. David Flusser of Hebrew University of Jerusalem, Dr. Moshe Bar-Asher of Hebrew University of Jerusalem, Dr. William Sanford LaSor, Professor emeritus at Fuller Theological Seminary, and Dr. Robert Lindsey.[20]

I agree with these scholars that Jesus indeed spoke Hebrew, not Aramaic. A key component in helping to analyze Jesus' utterance from the cross is to determine the everyday language of Jesus. The fact that Jesus' everyday spoken language was Hebrew is confirmed in Scripture.

Jesus Spoke Hebrew

Jesus spoke, read, and understood Hebrew. In Luke's Gospel, we are given a glimpse into Jesus' childhood. When Jesus was twelve years of age, his parents took him to Jerusalem to the feast of Passover. After the feast, on their return to Nazareth, Jesus' parents discovered that Jesus was not in their company of travelers. His parents returned to Jerusalem and searched for him.

Luke 2:46
46 And it came to pass, that after three days they found him in the temple, sitting in the midst of the doctors, both hearing them, and asking them questions.

In the Temple, the Old Testament Scriptures were only taught in Hebrew, by the doctors of the Law.[21] The facts that Jesus heard and understood the lessons taught by the doctors of the Law, prove that Jesus was very familiar with the Hebrew language. It is also apparent from this Scripture that Jesus conversed with the doctors of the Law. Verse forty-seven further corroborates Jesus' mastery of the Hebrew language.

Luke 2:47
47 And all that heard him were astonished at his understanding and answers.

Jesus' dialogue with the doctors of the Law required him to speak in the Hebrew language. His dialogue with the doctors of the Law, therefore, proves that Jesus both understood and spoke Hebrew.

From an early age, young Jewish boys were taught the Hebrew alphabet and taught to read the Hebrew Scriptures. Reader's Digest, "Jesus and His Times" states:

"The children literally sat at the feet of the teacher, who began by tracing out 22 letters of the Hebrew alphabet for them. After that, the children were introduced to individual words and then whole phrases from the Torah, their only "reading" material. But because Hebrew at the time was written without vowels, they could learn the sounds of the words only by listening to the teacher and repeating aloud after him."[22]

Some other scholars have propounded that Greek was the everyday language of Jesus. However, in his book, The Life and Times of Jesus the Messiah, Alfred Edersheim states:

"If Greek was the language of the court and camp, and indeed must have been understood and spoken by most in the land, the language of the people, spoken also by Christ and his Apostles was a dialect of the ancient Hebrew, the Western or

Palestinian Aramaic. It seems strange, that this could ever have been doubted. A Jewish Messiah Who would urge His claim upon Israel in Greek, seems almost a contradiction in terms. We know, that the language of the temple and the Synagogue was Hebrew, and that the addresses of the Rabbis had to be 'targumed' into the vernacular Aramaean---and can we believe that, in a Hebrew service, the Messiah could have addressed the people in Greek, or that He would ever argue with the Pharisees and Scribes in that tongue, especially remembering that its study was actually forbidden by the Rabbis."[23]

Since we know that Hebrew was the language of the Temple, we can deduce that the "doctors" spoke in Hebrew on the days that Jesus was in the Temple. In addition, the facts that Jesus heard the doctors of the Law ("both hearing them") and asked them questions ("and asking them questions"), indicate that Jesus both understood and spoke the Hebrew Language.

Jesus Spoke Hebrew in the synagogue

Another Scriptural example of Jesus speaking Hebrew is recorded in the Gospel of Luke. In the following text, Jesus is reading from the Hebrew Scriptures and speaking to a Hebrew congregation. Jesus would have spoken the language of the people of Nazareth, the town where he grew up.

Luke 4:15-22
15 And he taught in their synagogues, being glorified of all.
16 And he came to Nazareth, where he had been brought up: And, as his custom was, he went into the synagogue on the sabbath day, and stood up for to read.

17 And there was delivered unto him the book of the Prophet Esaias. And when he had opened the book, he found the place where it was written,

18 The Spirit of the Lord is upon me, because he hath anointed me to preach the gospel to the poor; he hath sent me to heal the brokenhearted, to preach deliverance to the captives, and recovering of sight to the blind, to set at liberty them that are bruised,

19 To preach the acceptable year of the Lord.

20 And he closed the book, and gave it again to the minister, and sat down. And the eyes of all them that were in the synagogue were fastened on him.

21 And he began to say unto them, this day is this scripture fulfilled in your ears.

22 And all bare him witness, and wondered at the gracious words which proceeded out of his mouth. And they said, Is not this Joseph's son?

During the time of Jesus, many countries and territories were Greek in culture. They had adopted the Greek culture and the Greek language. However, in areas in Judea and Galilee, Jewish culture was still dominant. In these Jewish towns and areas, Aramaic and Hebrew were still the dominant languages.[24]

The Old Testament Scriptures were written in Hebrew. Passages from these Hebrew Scriptures were read in the synagogues each Sabbath. In synagogues where Hebrew was not the common language, people could not understand the Scriptures that were read in Hebrew. Synagogues, however, found a solution to this problem. Synagogues would use persons who understood Hebrew, to translate the Hebrew text into the common language of the congregation. After Scripture verses were read in Hebrew, the translator, standing beside the reader, would translate what had been read in Hebrew.[25]

After reading from the Scriptures, Jesus sat down. There is no mention of a translator, translating to the congregation what Jesus had read from the Hebrew Scriptures. This shows that a translator was not needed to translate to the people what Jesus had read. This fact, in turn, shows that the people understood Hebrew, because after Jesus read from the Hebrew Scriptures, he taught the people without the need for a translator (Luke 4:21).

Alfred Edersheim further states, "That He [Jesus] spoke Hebrew, and used and quoted Scriptures in the original, has already been shown, although, no doubt, He [Jesus] understood Greek, possibly also Latin."[26]

Paul the Apostle Spoke Hebrew

The Book of Acts adds to the evidence that Jesus spoke in the Hebrew language. In recounting his conversion experience, Paul states that Jesus spoke Hebrew.

Acts 26:13-15

13 At midday, O king, I saw in the way a light from heaven, above the brightness of the sun, shining round about me and them which journeyed with me.

14 And when we were all fallen to the earth, I heard a voice speaking unto me, and saying in the **Hebrew** tongue, Saul, Saul, why persecutest thou me? It is hard for thee to kick against the pricks.

15 And I said, Who art thou, Lord? And he said, I am Jesus whom thou persecutest.

Paul (Saul, his Hebrew name) clearly states in verse fourteen that Jesus spoke to him in the Hebrew language. Paul did not say that Jesus spoke to him in the Greek language, nor in the Aramaic language. From this account, we can see that Paul, a contemporary of Jesus, also understood Hebrew. We, also, know from other Scriptures that Paul spoke Hebrew.

Acts 21:40; 22:1-2
40 And when he had given him licence, Paul stood on the stairs, and beckoned with the hand unto the people. And when there was made a great silence, he spake unto them in the **Hebrew** tongue, saying,
22 Men, brethren, and fathers, hear ye my defence which I make now unto you.
2 (And when they heard that he spake in the **Hebrew** tongue to them, they kept the more silence: and he saith,)

Not only did Paul understand Hebrew, he spoke Hebrew, because he spoke in Hebrew to the crowd of Jews in Jerusalem. If Aramaic or Greek was the everyday language of the Jews in the time of Jesus, as some scholars would have us to believe, why did Paul address the crowd in Hebrew?

It is true that during the time of Jesus, Israel and many countries had been conquered by the Roman Empire. As a result of Roman conquest, the Roman language (Latin) was adopted into the culture of many of these countries. Also, during the time of Jesus, many countries and territories had adopted the Greek culture, and had adopted the Greek language. Therefore, Greek and Latin are two of the predominant languages spoken during the time of Jesus. There is also archeological evidence that Greek and Latin were languages that were spoken by the gentiles (non-Jews) in Jesus' day. Archeologists have unearthed a stone with an inscription from the Temple (which was extant during the time of the ministry of Jesus), written in both Greek and Latin, which warned gentiles not to enter beyond a particular point.[27]

Another New Testament account that supports the fact that Hebrew was the language spoken by the Jews, and that Greek and Latin were the languages spoken by the populace is the superscription on the cross of Jesus. The superscription that was written and placed on the cross of Jesus was written in Greek, Latin and Hebrew (Luke. 23:38; Jn. 19:20). The Aramaic language is not included in the superscription.

The writings in the Dead Sea Scrolls discovered between 1947 and 1956 give additional historical evidence that Hebrew was an everyday language spoken by the Jews in the days of Jesus.[28] From the aforementioned sources of biblical evidence and biblical scholastic support, we can conclude that Hebrew was the dominant language spoken by the Jews in areas of Judea and Galilee, and that Hebrew was the everyday language spoken by Jesus. These two facts will be critically important in helping to explain that Jesus spoke in tongues when he was on the cross.

Jesus Spoke in an Unknown Tongue

Just as scholars are divided in their opinion of what language Jesus commonly spoke, they are equally divided in their opinion of what language Jesus spoke when he uttered "E'-li, E'-li, la'-ma sa-bach'-tha-ni?" from the cross. Many scholars agree that this utterance of Jesus was a combination of both Hebrew and

Aramaic. Surprisingly, we shall see from further study of the text that, what Jesus uttered and what is written are two separate phenomena.

What transpires in this verbal expression from the cross is what Paul calls "divers kinds of tongues" and "the interpretation of tongues" (1 Cor. 12:10). Kenneth E. Hagin in his book, The Holy Spirit and His Gifts, defines divers kinds of tongues as:

"Divers kinds of tongues is supernatural utterance by the Holy Spirit in languages never learned by the speaker, nor understood by the speaker, nor necessarily always understood by the hearer. Speaking with tongues has nothing whatsoever to do with linguistic ability; it has nothing to do with the mind or the intellect of man. It is a vocal miracle of the Holy Spirit."[29]

Mr. Hagin also elaborates further on the gift of the interpretation of tongues. He states:

"The gift of interpretation of tongues is the least gift of all the gifts of the Spirit because it depends upon another gift --- divers kinds of tongues --- in order to operate. It does not operate unless tongues have been in operation. The purpose of the gift of interpretation of tongues is to render the gift of tongues understandable to the hearers so that the whole church congregation, as well as the one who gave the utterance in the unknown tongue, may know what has been said and may be edified thereby."[30]

Speaking in divers kinds of tongues and the interpretation of tongues are two of the nine gifts of the Holy Spirit. Paul lists these gifts in the twelfth chapter of First Corinthians. He writes:

1 Corinthians 12:7-11

7 But the manifestation of the Spirit is given to every man to profit withal.

8 For to one is given by the Spirit the word of wisdom; to another the word of knowledge by the same Spirit;

9 To another faith by the same Spirit; to another the gifts of healing by the same Spirit;

10 To another the working of miracles; to another prophesy; to another discerning of spirits; to another divers kinds of tongues; to another the interpretation of tongues:

11 But all these worketh that one and the selfsame Spirit, dividing to every man severally as he will.

These nine gifts of the Spirit are endowments of God's power and abilities that God has given to the Church to profit the body of Christ. Under the Old Covenant, all of these gifts, excluding divers kinds of tongues and the interpretation of tongues, operated in various men and women of God, as God willed. The gifts of divers kinds of tongues and the interpretation of tongues first manifested in operation in the ministry of Jesus. Moreover, all of these various gifts still operate in the Church today, through various Spirit-filled believers, as the Spirit wills. However, in order to see a greater manifestation of the operation of these gifts of the Spirit, we are commanded by Paul to, "covet earnestly the best gifts (1 Cor. 12:31a).

As the head of the Church, Jesus ministered in all nine gifts of the Holy Ghost. Furthermore, we have learned from studying the Scriptures that even though Jesus was God, he did not ministered on earth as Almighty God. Jesus ministered on earth as a man filled with the Holy Ghost, who operated in the gifts of the Holy Ghost.

These gifts were not in constant manifestation in Jesus' life or ministry. These gifts began to operate in Jesus' ministry only after he was baptized in the Holy Ghost (Jn. 2:11). Again, it is important to remember that these gifts operated in the ministry of Jesus only as God willed, not as Jesus willed.

By using his own will, Jesus could not go to the graveyard and resurrect persons who had died that day or any other day. The gifts operated only as the Father willed. Neither could Jesus, by his own will, tell what any person in his presence was thinking. The gifts operated only when and how the Father willed.

Jesus was God Eternal, Who birthed Himself into the world, void of His divine power (Phil.2:7). Since Jesus was born void of all divine power, it was impossible for him to perform any supernatural acts on his own accord. Jesus could not operate the spiritual gifts as he willed. In the ministry of Jesus, Jesus was totally dependent upon his Father, Who operated the gifts of the Spirit through him, as the Father willed.

Therefore, no miracle in the New Testament was actually a miracle of Jesus. Every miracle in Jesus' ministry was in actuality a manifestation of one or more of the nine gifts of the Spirit in operation, as God willed. The miracles of Jesus are actually the works of God, using the operations of the gifts of the Spirit to operate in the ministry of Jesus. When Jesus stated, in John, chapter fourteen, that "the Father that dwelleth in me, he doeth the works," he was referring to God working through him, as God willed, through the operation of the nine gifts of the Holy Spirit.

The works of God were wrought through Jesus, who ministered through the various manifestations and operations of the nine gifts of the Holy Spirit. Jesus' utterance from the cross, "E'-li, E'-li, la'-ma sa-bach'-tha-ni?" is a clear manifestation of the operation of the gift of the interpretation of tongues. The actual words that Jesus spoke in tongues from the cross are not recorded. The words, "My God, my God, why hast thou forsaken me?" are simply a "targum" (translation) of the words "E'-li, E'-li, la'-ma sa-bach'-tha-ni?" In short, Jesus spoke in tongues on the cross and after his ascension, interpreted and revealed the interpretation of the utterance to two of the Gospel writers (Matthew and Mark). (The facts that Jesus received the interpretation of the utterance from God, and later revealed the interpretation to Matthew and Mark, illustrate the manifestation of the gift of the interpretation of tongues.) These writers, inspired by the Holy Ghost, recorded the interpretation and made it available to the entire Church to profit withal. Therefore, Jesus did minister in both tongues and interpretation. This can be illustrated from the Scripture text.

The interpretation of tongues can be simply defined as a supernatural interpretation of an utterance spoken in tongues. The interpretation is not the utterance; it is a supernatural interpretation of the utterance. Therefore, if an utterance in tongues is interpreted and written down, the interpretation is written down, but the actual utterance is not written down. It is not possible to write down the actual utterance in tongues because the words are "inaudible," that is, the words are "unintelligible." The Spirit inspired interpretation of an utterance in tongues can be written down in a known language, however, the actual utterance in unknown tongues cannot be written down, because the utterance in tongues is in an unknown language (which makes it unintelligible).

The utterance that Jesus spoke was "unintelligible" because it was spoken in an unknown tongue (language). The supernatural interpretation of the utterance that Jesus spoke is what Matthew and Mark record in their Gospels (Matt. 27:4; Mk. 15:34).

Jesus clearly spoke this utterance in an unknown tongue, because none of the Hebrew or Aramaic speaking Jews in the crowd understood what Jesus said. In fact, not a single person in the entire crowd understood this utterance, even though Jesus spoke it in a loud voice (Matt. 27:46a). We have previously shown that Hebrew was the everyday language of both Jesus and the Jews of Judea and Galilee. If Jesus had spoken this utterance in Hebrew, a common language of the Jews, the Hebrew speaking Jews would have readily understood that Jesus was quoting from the twenty-second Psalm.

Psalm 22:1
1 My God, my God, why hast thou forsaken me? why art thou so far from helping me, and from the words of my roaring?

Many Jewish religious leaders would have been present at Jesus' crucifixion, including chief priests, priests, doctors of the law, scribes, Pharisees and Sadducees. Certainly these religious leaders had knowledge of the Hebrew Scriptures. They would have understood what Jesus said, if Jesus had uttered those words in Hebrew. Yet, not a single religious leader, doctor of the law, Jew, gentile, sinner or saint understood a single word of Jesus' utterance.

This utterance from the cross is a clear illustration of Jesus speaking in other tongues. The Apostle Paul's definition of speaking in other tongues in chapter fourteen of First Corinthians, illustrates this point very clearly. Paul states, "For he that speaketh in an unknown tongue speaketh not unto men, but unto God: for no man understandeth him: howbeit in the spirit he speaketh mysteries (1 Cor. 14:2).

Paul's definition of speaking in unknown tongues consists of the following four factors. He that speaketh in an unknown tongue: (1) "speaketh not unto men," (2) "but unto God," (3) "for no man understandeth him," and (4) "howbeit in the spirit he speaketh mysteries." According to Paul's definition, an utterance would have to include all four factors in order to be defined as a supernatural utterance in unknown tongues.

Jesus' utterance from the cross fulfills all four of Paul's factors that constitute speaking in tongues. The first factor that Jesus's utterance fulfills is that it was not spoken unto men. This can be determined from Matthew's and Mark's recorded translation of Jesus' utterance, "My God, my God, why hast thou forsaken me?" It is obvious that Jesus was not addressing any segment of humanity.

The second factor of Paul's definition of unknown tongues that Jesus' utterance fulfills is that it was spoken unto God. The interpretation, "My God, my God, why hast thou forsaken me?" shows specifically that God, not humanity, was the intended recipient of Jesus' cry.

The third factor that Jesus' utterance fulfills is that no one understood the words that Jesus spoke. The Gospel writers record that Jesus spoke his utterance in a loud voice. Therefore, it is clear from Scripture that the people heard what Jesus said, yet they did not understand what he said. Matthew and Mark record:

Matthew 27:47
47 Some of them that stood there, when they **heard that**, said, This man calleth for Elias.

Mark 15:35
35 And some of them that stood by, when they **heard it**, said, Behold, he calleth Elias.

Paul states, "for no man understandeth him." The fact that the people thought Jesus was calling for Elias illustrates they did not understand what Jesus said.

The fourth factor of Paul's definition of unknown tongues that is contained in Jesus' utterance is, Jesus' utterance was a mystery. Jesus spoke seven different times from the cross (Matt. 27:46; Lk. 23:34; Lk. 23:43; Lk. 23:46; Jn. 19:26-27; Jn. 19:28; Jn. 19:30). All of the utterances from the cross were in understandable speech, except this unique utterance. The crowd thought that this utterance was a plea from Jesus for help from the prophet Elias. In actuality, the utterance was not a plea to the prophet for help, but a question to God for an answer. The fact that the utterance was heard, but its meaning was not understood, emphasizes the fact that the utterance was a mystery. Paul states, "howbeit in the spirit he speaketh mysteries."

This particular cry of Jesus from the cross was "inaudible," that is, the words were heard, but they were unintelligible. These words spoken by Jesus can also be referred to as "groaned in the spirit" (Jn. 11:33), "groaning in himself" (Jn. 11:38), and "groanings which cannot be uttered" (Rom. 8:26). Jesus spoke an inaudible question to God in an unknown tongue.

Jesus operated in the Gifts of the Spirit

As previously recorded, the list of the nine gifts of the Holy Spirit includes: (1) the word of wisdom; (2) the word of knowledge; (3) faith; (4) the gifts of healing; (5) the working of miracles; (6) prophecy; (7) discerning of spirits; (8) divers kinds of tongues; and (9) the interpretation of tongues (1 Cor. 12:8-10). These gifts are supernatural manifestations of the power and abilities of God. They are given by God to the Church to operate through various believers in the Church, as the Spirit wills. God gives different gifts to different people. God then operates these various gifts through the willing cooperation of the various believers. Believers do not operate these gifts when and how they choose, these gifts operate in the believer only when and how God wills, with the believers' cooperation.

Because Jesus was the head of the body of Christ, he operated in all nine gifts of the Spirit. However, the nine gifts of the Spirit were not in constant operation in the life of Jesus. Jesus did not walk around twenty-four hours a day operating in the spiritual gifts. Except for the times when God operated certain gifts through Jesus, Jesus' knowledge and power were as limited as any normal person's knowledge and power are limited. Particular gifts operated at various times in the life of Jesus, as the Spirit willed. Jesus operated in the gifts as he was empowered and led of God.

The Gift of Divers Kinds of Tongues

The gift of divers (various) kinds of tongues is one of the nine supernatural gifts that God has given to the Church. Since Jesus ministered at various times through each of the nine gifts of the Spirit, he would have at some time ministered in the gift of divers kinds of tongues. It is important that we understand the operation of this gift. This gift is exercised when a Spirit-filled believer is empowered and prompted by the Holy Spirit to speak a communication to the Church in a language that is unknown to the speaker, and usually unknown to the hearers. This gift, as well as the other eight spiritual gifts, is meant for public ministry. This means that God uses believers to minister to the body of Christ (the Church) using the operation of these gifts in public settings.

In this study, it is important to understand that there are two distinct classifications or manifestations of speaking in tongues. One manifestation of speaking in tongues is called "the simple gift of tongues." The other manifestation of speaking in tongues is called "the gift of divers kinds of tongues." In both manifestations (the simple gift of tongues and the gift of divers kinds of tongues), a Spirit-filled believer speaks in tongues, however, the purpose and the functions of the two types of tongues are uniquely different. The purpose and function of the simple gift of tongues is different from the purpose and function of the gift of divers kinds of tongues.

All Spirit filled believers receive the ability to speak in the simple gift of tongues when they are initially baptized in the Holy Ghost (Acts 2:4). The simple gift of tongues is given to every Spirit-filled believer to exercise at his or her own will, for private devotions and worship of God. Praying in the simple gift of tongues also builds up the spirit of the believer (Jude 20). The simple gift of tongues is not intended for public ministry in the Church. Also, the simple gift of tongues is usually not interpreted. When a Spirit-filled believer speaks in the simple gift of tongues, God usually does not give the speaker an interpretation of the tongues that were spoken. Again, this is because the simple gift of tongues is for private self-ministry and ministry to God.

The simple gift of tongues is not one of the nine public ministry gifts that are mentioned in First Corinthians, chapter twelve (1 Cor. 12:8-10). When Paul asks in First Corinthians, chapter twelve, "Do all speak with tongues?", Paul is referring to the public ministry gift of divers kinds of tongues. Paul was asking, "Do all Spirit-filled believers possess the gift of divers kinds of tongues (the public ministry gift)?" The answer is, No. Not many Spirit-filled believers will possess the gift of divers kinds of tongues. God will use only a nominal number of Spirit-filled believers to minister publically using the gift of divers kinds of tongues. However, all Spirit-filled believers do possess the simple gift of tongues and can minister privately to themselves and to God, whenever and wherever they choose.

In contrast to the simple gift of tongues, the gift of divers (various) kinds of tongues is one of the nine public ministry gifts that are named in First Corinthian, chapter twelve. The gift of divers kind of tongues is intended for public ministry in the Church. The gift of divers kinds of tongues is operated as the Spirit wills, not as the Spirit-filled believer wills. All Spirit-filled believers have the ability to speak in the simple gift of tongues. However, God alone chooses when, where and through which Spirit-filled believer He will operate the gift of divers kind of tongues. Also, unlike the simple gift of tongues, an utterance that is spoken in divers kinds of tongues is usually followed by an interpretation (the gift of the interpretation of tongues). Sometimes God anoints the person who spoke the utterance to interpret the meaning of the utterance, in a language that is usually understood by the speaker and the public assembly. At other times, God will anoint any of the various Spirit-filled believers in the assembly to interpret publically the meaning of the utterance.

Not knowing the distinction and purpose of these two kinds of tongues is what caused confusion in the Corinthian church in Paul's day (1 Cor. 14:1-33), and is still causing confusion in the present day Church. Because Spirit-filled believers can speak in the simple gift of tongues whenever and wherever they will, in Paul's day, some of the Spirit-filled believers tried to minister publically using their simple gift of tongues. This is not the purpose of the simple gift of tongues. The simple gift of tongues should not be used to try to minister publically in the Church. The simple gift of tongues should only be used for the private devotions and self-ministry of the speaker. It is God's prerogative to decide which Spirit-filled believer(s) He will use to minister in the gift of divers kinds of tongues in public settings (1 Cor. 14:27-33).

It is also important to note, Paul did not forbid believers from speaking in tongues in the church services, he only forbade believers from trying to use the simple gift of tongues to minister publically (1 Cor. 14:39). The simple gift of tongues is not for public ministry. Paul, however, wanted Spirit-filled believers to continue ministering to themselves and to God, using the simple gift of tongues. And, he told the Church to stop forbidding believers to speak in other tongues. He writes, "Wherefore, brethren, covet to prophesy, and **forbid not to speak with tongues** (1 Cor. 14:39).

Each gift of the Holy Ghost is supernatural, because it is an exercise of the power of God. Each public ministry gift (the nine gifts of the Spirit) is exercised as the Spirit wills, through the cooperation of a Spirit-filled believer. In other words, the Holy Ghost does not take control of an individual and force that individual to do a particular action. Paul states, "And the spirits of the prophets are subject to the prophets" (1 Cor. 14:32). By this, Paul indicates that the Holy Spirit does not operate by seizing control of an individual, or by overriding the will of an individual. The operations of the Holy Ghost are always under the believer's subjection. The believer always has the power to choose to cooperate with God's Spirit or choose not to cooperate with God's Spirit. The Amplified Bible is clearer in its translation of Paul's statement.

1 Corinthians 14:32 (The Amplified Bible)
32 For the spirits of the prophets [the speakers in tongues] are under the speaker's control [and subject to being silenced as may be necessary],

The utterance of Jesus from the cross was a supernatural utterance. He spoke as he was moved or prompted by the Holy Ghost to speak (Jn. 14:10). Remember, "divers kinds of tongues is supernatural utterance in an unknown tongue".[31]

The Manifestation of Divers Kinds of Tongues

The words "Eli, Eli, lama sabachthani" are the divinely inspired Word of God (Matt. 27:46b). Mark records this expression slightly differently from Matthew. Mark records "Eloi, Eloi, lama sabachthani" (Mk. 15:34b). Mark's recorded expression is also the divinely inspired Word of God. The Gospel writers wrote these words as the Holy Ghost inspired them to write.

Yet, even though the words "Eli, Eli, lama sabachthani" and the words "Eloi, Eloi, lama sabachthani" are divinely inspired; they never were spoken from the lips of Jesus as he hung on the cross. Mark makes it clear that these words are an interpretation of the utterance of Jesus, not the actual utterance itself.

Mark 15:34
34 And at the ninth hour Jesus cried with a loud voice saying, Eloi, Eloi, lama sabachthani? **which is being interpreted**, My God, my God, why hast thou forsaken me?

The words "Eloi, Eloi, lama sabachthani" and the words "Eli, Eli, lama sabachthani" are an interpretation of the words that Jesus spoke. The actual utterance that Jesus spoke was never recorded. What is recorded is the interpretation of Jesus' utterance and its translation! The words "My God, my God, why hast thou forsaken me?" are a translation of the words "Eloi, Eloi, lama sabachthani" and "Eli, Eli, lama sabachthani."

The actual utterance that Jesus spoke was in an unknown tongue. The Gospel writers (Matthew and Mark) do not record the actual utterance in tongues that Jesus spoke. They only record the interpretation of Jesus' utterance and its translation. The interpretation of Jesus' utterance is what is recorded in Scripture.

Merriam Webster's Collegiate Dictionary defines "interpret" as: to explain or tell the meaning of: present in understandable terms 2: to conceive in the light of individual belief, judgment, or circumstance : construe 3 : to represent by means of art : bring to realization by performance or direction: to act as an interpreter between speakers of different languages.[32]

Words spoken supernaturally in an unknown tongue are not understood by the speaker, nor usually by the hearers. God must therefore empower a Spirit-filled believer to operate in the gift of the interpretation of tongues, to speak in an understandable language, what was uttered in unknown tongues.

However, when Jesus spoke the utterance in unknown tongues, there were no Spirit-filled believers in existence, other than Jesus. This was because the gift of the Holy Spirit, in addition to the gift of divers (various) kinds of tongues and the gift of the interpretation of tongues were not given to the body of Christ (the Church) until after Jesus' ascension.[33] Because Jesus was praying to God (and not speaking to mankind), he could have simply uttered a prayer silently to God, for only God to hear. However, Jesus spoke the utterance in a loud voice (which was the gift of divers kinds of tongues), because God knew that the Church would later benefit from its interpretation. Thus, Matthew and Mark were later given its interpretation to reveal to the Church. However, all of the people present at Jesus' crucifixion left the crucifixion not knowing the meaning of Jesus' utterance. Jesus states in John, chapter sixteen:

John 16:13-14

13 Howbeit when he, the Spirit of truth, is come, he will guide you into all truth: for he shall not speak of himself; but whatsoever he shall hear, that shall he speak: and he will shew you things to come.

14 He shall glorify me: for he shall receive of mine, and shall shew it unto you.

The following two facts are further proof that Jesus spoke the utterance in an unknown tongue. First, no one in the crowd understood the meaning of the utterance, even though it was distinctly heard. Jesus uttered it in a loud voice. Second, the utterance had to be interpreted through the divine revelation of Jesus, through the Holy Spirit.

Jesus was sent by God to do public ministry. His utterance from the cross was not spoken to himself, nor was it spoken quietly. Jesus' utterance from the cross was spoken loudly, and it required an interpretation. This illustrates that Jesus spoke in divers (various) kinds of tongues. In addition, Matthew records Jesus' utterance in a combination of two different tongues or languages (both Hebrew and Aramaic) --- which symbolizes that Jesus' utterance was in divers (various) kinds of tongues.

Also, the composition or makeup of the crowd at the crucifixion further corroborates that Jesus spoke the utterance in tongues. First, Mary (the mother of Jesus) and John (the disciple of Jesus) were standing at the cross that day. Mary is representative of the language that Jesus was taught to speak from childhood. As Jesus' mother, Mary would have helped to teach Jesus to speak his basic common language. Therefore, if Jesus had spoken this utterance in his basic common language, certainly Mary would have understood the utterance of her own child. However, Mary did not understand the utterance.

Next, John (Jesus' disciple) was standing with Mary. John represents the language in which his rabbi, Jesus, taught. Jesus had a public ministry that spanned almost three and one-half years. John was there possibly every day hearing Jesus teach. If Jesus had spoken his utterance in the language in which he taught, certainly John standing at the cross would have understood the language of his Master. However, neither did John understand the utterance.

Roman soldiers who crucified Jesus also stood near the cross. These Roman soldiers spoke Latin, in addition, some spoke Greek, along with some of the Jews. If Jesus had spoken his utterance in Latin or in Greek, some of the soldiers or some of the Jews would have understood him. However, none of the people understood Jesus' utterance.

In Matthew's gospel the words "Eli, Eli" are Hebrew. The remainder of the interpretation "lama sabachthani?" is words in Aramaic. In Mark's gospel, the entire interpretation "Eloi, Eloi, lama sabachthani?" is words in Aramaic.[34] Hebrew and Aramaic are two languages that were commonly spoken by the Jews, yet no Jews in the crowd understood the utterance. Many readers of these Scripture passages assume that the words "Eloi, Eloi, lama sabachthani?" (Mk. 15:34b) and "Eli, Eli, lama sabachthani?" (Matt. 27:46b) are the actual words that Jesus uttered from the cross. However, Mark shows that the words that are recorded in this Scripture passage are an interpretation of Jesus' actual unrecorded utterance.

Mark records, "when they heard it" (Mk. 15:35b). The "it" that Mark records that they heard cannot be "Eloi, Eloi, lama sabachthani?" because "Eloi, Eloi, lama sabachthani?" is a known language (Aramaic) of the Jews and would not need to be interpreted through the unction of the Holy Ghost. Intelligible human languages are translated into other languages; they are not interpreted. The utterance that Jesus spoke from the cross was interpreted through the unction of the Holy Ghost, indicating that it was not spoken in an intelligible human language. On the other hand, the accuracy of the recorded translation "My God, my God, why hast thou forsaken me?" is not an issue. Both Matthew and Mark record the translation the same.

Because "My God, my God, why hast thou forsaken me?" is a translation of the interpretation "Eli, Eli, lama sabachthani?" the actual utterance is not known. In other words: (A) Jesus spoke an utterance in an unknown tongue. (B) The interpretation of the utterance (not the actual utterance) is recorded as "Eli, Eli, lama sabachthani?" (C) The interpretation "Eli, Eli, lama sabachthani?" is translated as "My God, my God, why hast thou forsaken me?" We can see from this sequence that (B) the interpretation of the utterance is recorded ("Eli, Eli, lama sabachthani?"). We can see that (C) the translation of the interpretation is recorded ("My God, my God, why hast thou forsaken me?"). And, we can see that (A) the actual utterance in unknown tongues is not recorded. The actual utterance that came from Jesus' lips is not known, because the utterance was spoken in an unknown tongue.

By recording the words "Eli, Eli, lama sabachthani?" in a composite language of Hebrew and Aramaic, the Holy Spirit is again indicating that these are not the exact words that came from Jesus' mouth. Jesus would never have spoken this Psalm in such a manner (Ps.22:1a). Jesus was the Word of God made flesh. The Law and the Prophets were written in Hebrew. Jesus came to fulfill the Law and the Prophets (Mt. 5:17). As teachers of the Law were required by the Law to teach the Scriptures only in Hebrew, Jesus would not have uttered this Hebrew Psalm unto God in a composite language of Hebrew and Aramaic (Matt. 27:46), nor in complete Aramaic (Mk. 15:34).[35]

CHAPTER 7

The Promise of the Spirit

Is it important for us to be filled with the Holy Ghost and to speak in tongues? How important is it? It is of supreme importance, because Jesus required his mother, Mary, to be filled with the Holy Ghost and to speak with other tongues. Mary, the mother of our Lord and Savior, Jesus Christ, was filled with the Holy Ghost and spoke in other tongues.

It seems that Jesus should have been able to exempt his loving mother from such a requirement. She gave birth to him. She nursed him. She helped to rear him. She loved him. She was his mother. Surely, Jesus would exempt his mother from having to receive the Holy Spirit, would he not? The answer is NO. God required the same for Mary as He does for everyone else. God is no respecter of persons (Acts 10:34).

Jesus had brothers and sisters also. Jesus was not an only child. Matthew records:

Matthew 13:55-56 (The Living Bible)
55 "How is this possible?" the people exclaimed. "He's just a carpenter's son, and we know Mary his mother and his brothers---James, Joseph, Simon, and Judas.
56 And his sisters---they all live here. How can he be so great?"

The Bible records that Jesus' brothers became his disciples (Acts 1:14c). Surely, Jesus would have exempted his brothers from the requirements of receiving the Holy Ghost and speaking with other tongues, would he not? The answer again is, NO. Jesus did not exempt his brothers from these requirements. They too were required by Jesus to receive the baptism of the Holy Ghost and speak in other tongues.

Jesus also personally chose twelve disciples, which followed him day and night during his earthly ministry. They were Jesus' best students, with the exception of Judas Iscariot, who later committed suicide (Mt. 27:5). Surely, Jesus would not require his twelve intimate disciples, including Matthias, who replaced Judas Iscariot (Acts 1:26), to receive the Holy Ghost and to speak in other tongues. Jesus, however, did not exempt even his own close disciples from the requirements of receiving the Holy Ghost and speaking in other tongues. All of them: Jesus' mother, Jesus' brothers, and Jesus' twelve disciples were all filled with the Holy Ghost and spoke in other tongues.

Can you imagine Mary, the mother of Jesus, speaking in tongues? Can you imagine John, the beloved disciple, speaking in tongues? Can you imagine all of the twelve disciples speaking in tongues? Can you imagine approximately one hundred and twenty believers in the Upper Room receiving the baptism of the Holy Ghost and speaking in tongues? Luke records how it happened in the Book of Acts.

Acts 1:13-14; 2:1-4 (The Amplified Bible)
13 And when they had entered [the city], they mounted to the upper room where they were indefinitely staying --- **Peter** and **John** and **James** and **Andrew**, **Philip** and **Thomas**,

Bartholomew and **Matthew, James** the son of Alphaeus and **Simon** the Zealot and **Judas** the [son] of James.

14 All of these with their minds in full agreement devoted themselves steadfastly to prayer, [waiting together] with the **women** and **Mary** the mother of Jesus, and with His **brothers**.

2 And when the day of Pentecost had fully come, they were **all** assembled together in one place,

2 When suddenly there came a sound from heaven like the rushing of a violent tempest blast, and it filled the whole house in which they were sitting.

3 And there appeared to them tongues representing fire, which were separated and distributed and that settled on each one of them.

4 And they were **all filled** --- diffused throughout their souls --- with the Holy Spirit and began to speak in other (different, foreign) languages, as the Spirit kept giving them clear and loud expression (in each tongue in appropriate words).

Yes, Mary was there. John was there. The other disciples were there. Jesus' brothers were there. All were speaking in other tongues, along with more than one hundred other disciples.

Even though Mary had a unique relationship with Jesus, as his mother, her relationship did not exempt her from God's requirement of receiving the baptism of the Holy Spirit. Even though John had a unique relationship with Jesus, as the "disciple whom Jesus loved," his relationship did not exempt him from God's requirement of receiving the baptism of the Holy Spirit. Also, even though the disciples had a unique relationship with Jesus, as his closest followers, their relationship did not exempt them from God's requirement of receiving the baptism of the Holy Spirit. Jesus did not exempt a single person from God's requirement of receiving the baptism of the Holy Spirit. He told them all to go to Jerusalem and wait for the promise of the Holy Ghost (Jn. 7:39).

On the day of Pentecost, God sent the Holy Ghost to reside on the earth. By coming to earth as the Holy Spirit, God made Himself accessible to all of humanity. This means that the Holy Spirit is everywhere on earth today, and He is available to everyone who will receive Him.

Jesus, who was God (and who ministered on earth in his flesh and blood body), was limited in his range of accessibility to humanity. He could only be in one place at a time. In addition, Jesus was limited to walking among humanity and walking with humanity. However, after God the Holy Spirit came to earth, humanity's accessibility to God became infinite. (The Shekinah glory of God no longer remained centralized in the Temple in Jerusalem, which also limited the Jews' accessibility to God.) The coming of the Holy Ghost offered all believers everywhere unlimited access to God's presence. Not only could God the Holy Ghost be among believers, He could now dwell in the hearts of believers. Moreover, God the Holy Ghost was not limited to time and place. He could be everywhere on earth at the same time.

In this study we have learned that Jesus is the head of the Church (Eph. 5:23). He is the head of the body of Christ (Col. 1:18). As the head of the Church, Jesus received the baptism of the Holy Spirit and spoke in other tongues. We, the body of Christ on earth, are required to follow Jesus, the head of the Church. Can we followers of Christ say that we are following Jesus when we refuse to receive the same experience that he commanded his mother, brothers, and all of his disciples (the Church) to receive?

We are Forgiven

Through the sacrificial death of Jesus on the cross, once and for all, the penalty for the sins of humanity was paid for and abolished. By faith in the Lord Jesus Christ, the sins of repentant sinners are forgiven by God and washed away. Through the work of the Holy Spirit the human spirit (heart) of repentant sinners is born again and made into the image of their Savior, Jesus Christ (2 Cor. 5:17).

This is what happened to Mary, the mother of Jesus, and the other disciples in the Upper Room on the day of Pentecost. They were all born again spiritually and filled with the Holy Ghost and spoke in tongues. All of these actions are performed through the work of the Holy Ghost.

Before the sacrificial death of Jesus, the blood of sacrificial animals covered the sins of the Jews. However, after the sacrificial death of Jesus, the blood of Jesus paid the penalty for the sins of the whole world. Because Jesus paid mankind's sin debt, forgiveness of sins is offered to all humanity. Eternal life is given to every believer who by faith receive Jesus Christ as Savior and Lord (1 Jn. 5:10-12).

On the day of Pentecost, when Jewish onlookers heard Mary, the mother of Jesus, speaking in tongues, and the brothers of Jesus speaking in tongues, and all of the disciples speaking in tongues, they asked, "what does all of this mean?" In response to their question, Peter gave everyone a command. Luke records Peter's command.

Acts 2:38-39
38 Then Peter said unto them, Repent, and be baptized every one of you in the name of Jesus Christ for the remission of sins, and ye shall receive the gift of the Holy Ghost.

39 For the promise is unto you, and to your children, and to all that are afar off, even as many as the Lord our God shall call.

No longer is the blood of sacrificial animals required to allay the wrath of God for the punishment of the sins of humanity. The price of humanity's sin debt has been paid for with the blood of Jesus. Paul writes:

Hebrews 10:4-10
4 For it is not possible that the blood of bulls and of goats should take away sins.
5 Wherefore when he cometh into the world, he saith, Sacrifice and offering thou wouldest not, but a body hast thou prepared me:
6 In burnt offerings and sacrifices for sin thou hast no pleasure.
7 Then said I, Lo, I come (in the volume of the book it is written of me,) to do thy will, O God.
8 Above when he said, Sacrifice and offering and burnt offerings and offering for sin thou wouldest not, neither hadst pleasure therein; which are offered by the law;
9 Then said he, Lo, I come to do thy will, O God. He taketh away the first, that he may establish the second.
10 By the which will we are sanctified through the offering of the body of Jesus Christ once for all.

Sin no longer has to separate humanity from God. Through faith in the Lord Jesus Christ, we can receive total forgiveness for all of our sins. The total price for our past, present and future sin debt has been paid in full by Jesus. By asking God to forgive us of our sins, and asking Jesus to be our Savior and Lord, we can receive both forgiveness of sins and everlasting life. This experience is referred to in some Christian denominations as "to get saved" (Rom. 10:9) or "to be born again" (Jn. 3:3).

Mary, the mother of Jesus, had to do this. John had to do this. The brothers of Jesus had to do this. All of Jesus' disciples had to do this. They were possibly all nice, moral and religious people, who attended the synagogue regularly. The fact that they might have been nice, moral, religious churchgoers, did not exempt them from God's command. They still had to ask forgiveness for their sins, receive Jesus as their Savior and Lord, and receive the baptism of the Holy Spirit.

Dear reader, have you in like manner done what Mary, the mother of Jesus, did? Have you done what John did? Have you done what the brothers of Jesus did? Have you done what the disciples did? Have you asked God to forgive you of your sins? Have you asked Jesus to be your Salvation and Lord? Have you received the gift of the Holy Spirit? Have you demonstrated the biblical evidence that you are Spirit-filled, by speaking in other tongues, like Jesus, Mary, John, and the disciples did? If you answered "No" to any of these questions, you are missing some of God's greatest blessings for your life. Paul, writing under the anointing of the Holy Spirit, commanded the church in Ephesus:

Ephesians 5:18
18 And be not drunk with wine, wherein is excess; but be filled with the Spirit;

The Promise is for You

Several facts about the life of Jesus have been stated in this book. 1. Jesus was fully God, void of His divine powers, and He was born of the Spirit, fully human. 2. Jesus grew up as a normal child and was filled with the Holy Spirit at approximately age thirty. 3. Jesus kept himself spiritually charged by praying in other tongues. 4. Jesus ministered on earth as a Spirit-filled man, who operated in the gifts of the Spirit, as God the Father willed. 5. Jesus died sacrificially for the sins of the whole world.

What makes these facts even more great is, Jesus did all of these things for you and me. He not only died for our sins, he also lived a life that was pleasing to God, as a person filled with the Holy Spirit, in order to show us how to live our life pleasing to God. When Jesus received the baptism of the Holy Ghost, God voiced His approval by speaking from heaven. It is apparent that this event was important in the mind of God, because God inspired all four Gospel writers to record the event. The account in Matthew is typical of the other Gospel writers. Matthew records:

Matthew 3:16-17

16 And Jesus, when he was baptized, went up straightway out of the water: and, lo, the heavens were opened unto him, and he saw the Spirit of God descending like a dove, and lighting upon him: 17 And lo a voice from heaven, saying, This is my beloved Son, in whom I am well pleased.

The baptism in the Holy Ghost was not specifically for the early Church. Neither was speaking in tongues only for that time. After Jesus ascended back to heaven, God sent the Holy Ghost to the Church on the day of Pentecost, so that we too could do that which well pleases God, i.e., become spiritually born of the Spirit and spiritually filled with the Holy Ghost.

The baptism in the Holy Ghost was not just for Jesus. The baptism in the Holy Ghost was not just for Mary, the mother of Jesus. The baptism in the Holy Ghost was not just for the brothers of Jesus and for the disciples. Speaking in tongues was not just for Jesus. Speaking in tongues was not just for Mary, the mother of Jesus. Speaking in tongues was not just for the brothers of Jesus and his disciples. Speaking in tongues was not just for them in the early Church. These gifts are as available for us today as they were available for the early Church (Acts 2:39). These gifts were not given only to the early Church; neither did they pass away with the early Church.

Some people might think that the gift of tongues has passed away because Paul states, "tongues are for a sign." Let us examine what Paul really said.

1 Corinthians 14:21-22
21 In the law it is written, With men of other tongues and other lips will I speak unto this people; and yet for all that will they not hear me, saith the Lord.
22 Wherefore tongues are for a sign, not to them that believe, but to them that believe not: but prophesying serveth not for them that believe not, but for them which believe.

Paul states, "wherefore tongues are for a sign, not to them that believe, but to them that believe not." Here Paul is quoting from Isaiah, chapter twenty-eight, verses eleven and twelve, which state:

Isaiah 28:11-12
11 For with stammering lips and another tongue will he speak to this people.
12 To whom he said, This is the rest wherewith ye may cause the weary to rest; and this is the refreshing: yet they would not hear.

In Isaiah, God states that He will send the Jews a supernatural sign to call their attention back to the truth of His Word. The sign would be that God would send a people, who would speak to the Jews in unintelligible speech (a foreign tongue). Yet, God knew that the unbelieving Jews would not believe the sign. Isaiah records, "yet they would not hear." In First Corinthians 14:12, Paul is inferring that the occurrence of the disciples speaking in tongues on the day of Pentecost is the fulfillment of the sign referred to in Isaiah (Isa. 28:11) that God would send to unbelievers. God uses the act of speaking in other tongues as a sign to call unbelievers to repentance. It is a supernatural sign that God uses to call attention back to the truth of His Word. However, for Spirit-filled believers, speaking in other tongues is not for a sign, speaking in other tongues is a way of life. God still uses tongues (both the simple gift of tongues and the gift of divers kinds of tongues) and the gift of the interpretation of tongues, to speak through and to speak to His people, who are believers.

God sent the Holy Spirit on the day of Pentecost to indwell each of us, who receives Jesus as Lord and Savior. The Holy Ghost was not sent simply to indwell the Christians in the Upper Room. God sent the Holy Spirit so that we can all receive the gift of salvation and the gift of the Holy Ghost with the evidence of speaking in tongues. Dear readers, my questions to you are: Have you received the promise? Have you received the gift of salvation? Have you received the baptism of the Holy Spirit? Do you speak in other tongues? Today millions of Christians are like the "certain disciples" that Paul found in Ephesus.

Acts 19:1-2

1 And it came to pass, that, while Apollos was at Corinth, Paul having passes through the upper coasts came to Ephesus: and finding certain disciples,

2 He said unto them, Have ye received the Holy Ghost since ye believed? And they said unto him, We have not so much as heard whether there be any Holy Ghost.

These were believers ("disciples"), but they had never received the baptism of the Holy Spirit. When asked by Paul, "Have ye received the Holy Ghost since ye believed?", the disciples responded, "We have not so much as heard whether there be any Holy Ghost" (Acts 19:1-6). Does this story describe your experience? Are you like one of those disciples, whom no one has "found" and explained God's promise of the Holy Spirit? If so, you are as I was.

At the age of fourteen, I accepted Jesus Christ as my Savior and Lord. In my particular church denomination, this experience was called "being born again" or "being converted." I continued to attend church services in my denomination for sixteen years. I cannot remember any pastors who taught or preached on the importance of receiving the baptism of the Holy Spirit and speaking in other tongues. I did not know anyone in my denomination, who was filled with the Holy Ghost and who spoke in tongues.

At the age of twenty, I moved away from home in order to go to college. After earning my Bachelor's Degree, I earned a Master of Divinity Degree. Surprisingly, even in seminary, none of my professors taught me about the importance of receiving the baptism of the Holy Spirit and speaking in tongues. Therefore, I never sought these gifts.

After I graduated from seminary, I became a pastor of three small churches on a circuit. I never taught my congregations about the importance of receiving the infilling of the Holy Ghost and speaking in tongues. I could not teach what I did not know.

After pastoring for about two years, a change occurred in my life. I was introduced to an elderly Pentecostal pastor, who shared with me some of the Scriptures that I have shared in this book. He taught me about God's command to be filled with the Holy Spirit and to speak in tongues. Like Paul, he laid his hands on me and I received the baptism of the Holy Spirit and spoke in tongues. I thank God that some believers are staying true to God's Word. Now I teach and preach that God wants all of us to receive these same gifts. God's gifts are not earned. They are given freely to whomever will ask and receive them (Lk. 11:13).

The Realm of the Spirit Awaits You

When I was not yet a Spirit-filled Christian, I was only aware of the physical world in which I lived. However, when I became Spirit-filled and spoke in tongues, I became aware that a spirit world exists, that is as real as the natural world. God is a Spirit, and He lives in a spirit world. The spirit world opened up to Jesus immediately after he was filled with the Holy Ghost.

Matthew 3:16-17; 4:1-11
16 And Jesus, when he was baptized, went straightway out of the water: and lo, the heavens were opened unto him, and he saw the Spirit of God descending like a dove, and lighting upon him: 17 And lo a voice from heaven, saying, This is my beloved Son, in him I am well pleased.

4 Then was Jesus led up of the Spirit into the wilderness to be tempted of the devil.

2 And when he had fasted forty days and forty nights, he was afterward an hungered.

3 And when the tempter came to him, he said, If thou be the Son of God, command that these stones be made bread.

4 But he answered and said, It is written, Man shall not live by bread alone, but by every word that proceedeth out of the mouth of God.

5 Then the devil taketh him up into the holy city, and setteth him on a pinnacle of the temple.

6 And saith unto him, If thou be the Son of God, cast thyself down: for it is written, he shall give his angels charge concerning thee: and in their hands they shall bear thee up, lest at any time thou dash thy foot against a stone.

7 Jesus said unto him, It is written again, Thou shalt not tempt the Lord thy God.

8 Again, the devil taketh him up into an exceeding high mountain, and sheweth him all the kingdoms of the world, and the glory of them;

9 And saith unto him, All these things will I give thee, if thou wilt fall down and worship me.

10 Then saith Jesus unto him, Get thee hence, Satan: for it is written, Thou shalt worship the Lord thy God, and him only shalt thou serve.

11 Then the devil leaveth him, and, behold angels came and ministered unto him.

This experience in the life of Jesus illustrates that after a believer is filled with the Holy Ghost, the spirit world becomes more of a reality in his or her life. After Jesus was filled with the Holy Ghost these seven spiritual things happened.

1. God confirmed His relationship with Jesus by speaking from heaven.
2. Jesus was led of the Spirit into the wilderness.
3. Jesus fasted for forty days in the wilderness and prayed in tongues.
4. The existence of Satan became a reality in the life of Jesus.
5. The existence of angels became a reality in the life of Jesus.
6. The nine gifts of the Holy Spirit began to operate in Jesus' ministry.
7. Spiritual warfare became a reality in the life of Jesus.

Matthew writes in this same chapter:

Matthew 4:23-25

23 And Jesus went about all Galilee, teaching in their synagogues, and preaching the gospel of the kingdom, and healing all manner of sickness and all manner of disease among the people.

24 And his fame went throughout all Syria: and they brought unto him all sick people that were taken with divers diseases and torments, and those which were possessed with devils, and those which were lunatick, and those that had the palsy, and he healed them.

25 And there followed him great multitudes of people from Decapolis, and from Jerusalem, and from Judea and from beyond Jordan.

In the ministry of Jesus, we can see that the gifts of the Spirit began to operate, after he was filled with the Holy Spirit. For example, we can see the gifts of healing in operation when he healed the sick (Jn. 5:2-9). We can see the gift of working of miracles and the gift of faith operating when Jesus stilled the storm (Lk. 8:22-24). In addition, we can see the gift of discerning of spirits and the gift of faith in operation when he cast out devils (Mk. 5:1-13). The gifts of the Spirit can operate singularly or they can operate together in a variety of different combinations. As mentioned, the gift of working of miracles might work in combination with the gift of faith. The gift of the word of knowledge might operate together with the gifts of healing. The gift of divers kinds of tongues usually works in combination with the gift of the interpretation of tongues. God determines when, where, how, what and through whom the ministry gifts of the Holy Ghost are manifested.

The gift of salvation (Eph. 2:8), the gift of the Holy Ghost (Acts 2:38) and the nine gifts of the Spirit (1 Cor. 12:7-11) are as available for us today, as they were for the early Church. God has never removed these gifts from the Church. The gift of salvation and the gift of the Holy Ghost are received from God by faith. The nine gifts of the Spirit are given by God as He wills (1 Cor. 12:11) but, it is up to you and me to personally receive by faith the gifts of salvation and the gift of the Holy Ghost. Paul commands us to "covet earnestly the best gifts," (1 Cor. 12:31).

Ye Shall Receive Power

The power in Jesus' life resulted from the fact that Jesus was a man who was filled with the Holy Spirit and who prayed in tongues. Luke records:

Luke 1:34-35

34 Then said Mary unto the angel, How shall this be, seeing I know not a man?

35 And the angel answered and said unto her, The Holy Ghost shall come upon thee, and the power of the Highest shall overshadow thee: therefore also that holy thing which shall be born of thee shall be called the Son of God.

It was not enough that Jesus was born of the Spirit of God. After being born of the Spirit, Jesus had to take another step in order for him to continue to live a life that was pleasing unto God. Jesus had to receive the baptism in the Holy Spirit. Why was it necessary for Jesus to receive the baptism of the Holy Spirit? Here are five reasons why Jesus needed to be baptized in the Holy Ghost.

1. Jesus needed to be baptized in the Holy Ghost in order to be led of the Spirit.

Luke 4:1

1 And Jesus being full of the Holy Ghost returned from Jordan, and was led by the Spirit into the wilderness.

Romans 8:14

14 For as many as are led by the Spirit of God, they are the sons of God.

2. Jesus needed to be filled with the Holy Ghost in order to pray in the Spirit (speak in other tongues).

Luke 4:1-2, 14

4 And Jesus being full of the Holy Ghost returned from Jordan, and was led by the Spirit into the wilderness.

2 Being forty days tempted of the devil. And in those days he did eat nothing: and when they were ended, he afterward hungered.

14 And Jesus returned in the **power of the spirit** into Galilee: and there went out a fame of him through all the region round about.

Jesus assuredly prayed in tongues in the wilderness, because he returned in the power of the Spirit. He returned "edified" in the Spirit. Praying in other tongues is what spiritually edifies or builds up believers.

1 Corinthians 14:4

4 He that speaketh in an unknown tongue edifieth himself, but he that prophesieth edifieth the church.

Jude 20

20 But ye, beloved, building up yourselves on your most holy faith, praying in the Holy Ghost,

3.   Jesus needed to be filled with the Holy Spirit in order to operate in the power of God.

Matthew 9:8

8 But when the multitudes saw it, they marveled, and glorified God, which had given such power unto men.

Acts 1:8

8 But ye shall receive power, after that the Holy Ghost is come upon you: and ye shall be witnesses unto me both in Jerusalem, and in all Judaea, and in Samaria and unto the uttermost part of the earth.

4. Jesus needed to be filled with the Holy Ghost in order to operate in the nine gifts of the Holy Spirit, as the Spirit willed.

John 5:19, 30

19 Then answered Jesus and said unto them, Verily, verily, I say unto you, The Son can do nothing of himself, but what he seeth the Father do: for what things soever he doeth, these also doeth the Son likewise.

30 I can of mine own self do nothing: as I hear, I judge: and my judgment is just; because I seek not mine own will, but the will of the Father which hath sent me.

John 14:10

10 Believeth thou not that I am in the Father, and the Father in me? the words that I speak unto you I speak not of myself: but the Father that dwelleth in me, he doeth the works.

5. Jesus needed to be baptized in the Holy Ghost in order to fulfill the will of God.

John 8:29

29 And he that sent me is with me: the Father hath not left me alone; for I do always those things that please him.

John 4:38
38 For I came down from heaven, not to do mine own will, but the will of him that sent me.

Simply stated, Jesus needed to receive the baptism of the Holy Spirit and speak in other tongues in order to do the work of God and fulfill the will of God. Also, it is essential that every believer in the Church today receive the baptism of the Holy Spirit and speak in other tongues. This is necessary because, as the body of Christ, we too are called to do the work of God and fulfill the will of God.

Jesus Commanded His Disciples to be Filled with the Spirit

Are you a disciple of Jesus? Are you one of his followers? Jesus' command for his followers to be filled with the Holy Spirit was given to the entire assembly of believers, not simply to the eleven remaining disciples.

Luke 24:33, 36, 49
33 And they rose up the same hour, and returned to Jerusalem, and found the eleven gathered together, and them that were with them,
36 And as they thus spake, Jesus himself stood in the midst of them, and saith unto them, Peace be unto you.
49 And, behold, I send the promise of my Father upon you: but tarry ye in the city of Jerusalem, until ye be endued with power from on high.

Acts 1:4-5

4 And, being assembled together with them, commanded them that they should not depart from Jerusalem, but wait for the promise of the Father, which, saith he, ye have heard of me.

5 For John truly baptized with water, but ye shall be baptized with the Holy Ghost not many days hence.

We can see from these Scriptures that Jesus commanded everyone present to receive the baptism in the Holy Spirit, along with the eleven other disciples. God's command extends to all believers today to receive the baptism in the Holy Spirit.

Are You Ready?

On the day of Pentecost, God sent the Holy Spirit to minister on earth in the place of Jesus. Jesus said, "And I will pray the Father, and he shall give you another Comforter, that he may abide with you forever" (Jn. 14:16). Do you know the Comforter? Jesus said, "But the Comforter, which is the Holy Ghost, whom the Father will send in my name, he shall teach you all things, and bring all things to your remembrance, whatsoever I have said unto you" (Jn. 14:26). God, however, will never force the Holy Spirit upon any of us. It is our responsibility to **receive** the baptism in the Holy Spirit. Are you ready to **receive** Him? The following biblical accounts emphasize the fact that believers are to **receive** the Holy Ghost. God gave the Holy Ghost on the day of Pentecost; it is up to us to **receive** Him.

Acts 2:38

38 Then Peter said unto them, Repent, and be baptized every one of you in the name of Jesus Christ for the remission of sins, and ye shall **receive** the gift of the Holy Ghost.

Acts 8:15

15 Who, when they were come down, prayed for them, that they might **receive** the Holy Ghost.

Acts 10:45-47

45 And they of the circumcision which believed were astonished, as many as came with Peter, because that on the gentiles also was poured out the gift of the Holy Ghost.

46 For they heard them speak with tongues, and magnify God. Then answered Peter,

47 Can any man forbid water, that these should not be baptized, which have **received** the Holy Ghost as well as we?

Acts 19:2

2 He said unto them, Have ye **received** the Holy Ghost since ye believed? And they said unto him, We have not so much as heard whether there be any Holy Ghost.

In order to receive the infilling of the Holy Ghost, God requires that we first be born again (be saved). Are you born again? Jesus' command to Nicodemus in the Gospel of John is as necessary for us today as it was necessary in the time of Nicodemus. Jesus stated, "Marvel not that I said unto thee, Ye must be born again" (Jn. 3:7). Right now, by faith, you can receive Jesus Christ into your heart and receive salvation. You can become "born again." Read the following Scripture and prayer to see what is required of you to receive salvation.

Romans 10:9

9 That if thou shalt confess with thy mouth the Lord Jesus, and shalt believe in thine heart that God hath raised him from the dead, thou shalt be saved.

PRAYER:

Dear heavenly Father, You said in your Word, that if I confess with my mouth the Lord Jesus, and believe in my heart that God hath raised him from the dead, I shall be saved. I do believe in my heart that Jesus died on the cross for my sins. In addition, I do believe that he rose again from the dead on the third day.

I ask you, heavenly Father, to forgive me of all my sins, and cleanse me of all unrighteous. I invite Jesus to come into my heart right now and be my Salvation. I want to live for you, and do those things that are pleasing in thy sight. I confess Jesus now as my Salvation and Lord. And, according to your Word, I am now saved. Thank you Lord for saving me. In Jesus' name I pray. Amen.

Now that you have read the Scripture and prayer, if you desire to receive salvation, sincerely pray the prayer aloud to God, and God will save you. Please pray the prayer now.

CONGRADULATIONS, if you prayed the prayer, welcome to the family of God! You are now a child of God. You are now born of God's Spirit, and a new creature in Christ Jesus. Your old self has passed away (along with your sinful past), and now you are a new person in Christ Jesus--made in his image. Paul states, "Therefore if any man be in Christ, he is a new creature: old things are passed away; behold, all things are become new" (1Cor. 5:17).

Please note, your salvation experience should not be based on your feelings or upon other people's experiences. Not all people will weep and cry or have an experience as Paul had, when he received salvation (Acts 9:1-9). Our salvation is based on our faith in the Word of God, not on our feelings. Paul states, "For by grace are ye saved through faith; and that not of ourselves: it is the gift of God" (Eph. 2:8). Again, in his epistle to the Corinthians, Paul reminds us, "For we walk by faith, not by sight" (2 Cor. 5:7).

Fill Me with the Holy Spirit

Now that you are saved, do not stop at the salvation experience. Do what Jesus did, and receive the baptism in the Holy Spirit. Do you call Jesus Lord, and do not the things which he says (Lk. 6:46)? Jesus Christ was filled with the Holy Ghost and spoke in unknown tongues, and so can we. This is not a suggestion or recommendation from God, this is a command from Jesus, who is the Word of God (Lk. 24:49; Acts 3:38-39; Eph. 5:18).

Various scriptural accounts show that after various persons received the baptism in the Holy Spirit, they gave evidence that they were filled with the Holy Ghost by speaking in other tongues. It is very easy and simple to receive the infilling of the Holy Spirit and to speak in other tongues. Right now, you are only one prayer away. In order to receive the baptism in the Holy Spirit, each recipient must participate in the experience.

They Spake with Tongues

When God fills believers with the Holy Spirit, He gives them the ability to speak in other tongues. However, the individual believer must do the actual speaking in other tongues. In other words, the Holy Ghost does not take over a person's voice and start speaking in tongues. The Holy Ghost does not speak in tongues; the believer must do the actual speaking in tongues.

It is erroneous to think that the Holy Ghost will take control of our mouth and speak in tongues through us. The false belief that the Holy Ghost will speak in tongues through us has prevented many believers from entering into the fullness of the Spirit. Many sincere believers have asked God to fill them with the Holy Ghost, and have sat and waited for God to start speaking in tongues through them, and nothing has happened. Unfortunately, nothing will ever happen, because God does not speak in tongues through us, **we** speak in tongues through God. That is, God gives **us** the ability to speak in tongues, but **we** must do the actual speaking. Look at these examples in Scripture. In each example, the individual persons did the actual speaking in other tongues. It was not the Holy Ghost that did the speaking.

Acts 2:4
4 And they were all filled with the Holy Ghost, and **[they] began to speak** with other tongues, as the Spirit gave them utterance.

Acts 2:4 (New International Version)
4 All of them were filled with the Holy Spirit and **[they] began to speak** in other tongues as the Spirit enabled them.

Acts 10:46
46 For they heard **them speak** with tongues, and magnify God. Then answered Peter,

Acts 19:6
6 And when Paul had laid his hands upon them, the Holy Ghost came on them; and **they spake** with tongues, and prophesied.

Notice in all of these examples of people receiving the baptism of the Holy Ghost, it was the persons that did the speaking in other tongues, not the Holy Ghost. We, the individuals, are the ones who must do the speaking in other tongues. The Holy Ghost does not speak in tongues through us. The Holy Ghost enables **us** to do the speaking in tongues, that is, He gives **us** the supernatural ability to speak in other tongues. Every individual believer must do the actual speaking in tongues.

The Holy Ghost never takes control of our vocal cords and forces us to speak in tongues. Every one of us controls our own vocal cords. If we meet someone on the street and we want to say "Good morning," we must do the speaking. Similarly, after we receive the baptism of the Holy Ghost, if we want to speak in tongues, we must do the speaking.

Speaking in tongues is an act of faith. If we want to speak in tongues, we must act in faith. Faith is belief in the Word of God that is based on the Word's integrity. Paul states, "Now faith is the substance of things hoped for, the evidence of things not seen" (Heb. 11:1). In short, faith is acting like the Word of God is true. So, when we pray and ask God to fill us with the Holy Spirit, we must believe by faith that we receive the Holy Spirit. Then by faith, we must willfully begin to speak out of our mouth, syllables or words that the Holy Spirit enables us to speak. We will have no idea what the words will sound like until we speak them out aloud. We speak in tongues by our faith in the integrity of the Word of God. We speak in tongues by faith, knowing that God will not give us something that is evil. Jesus gives us this assurance in the Gospel of Luke:

Luke 11:9-13

9 And I say unto you, Ask, and it shall be given you; seek, and ye shall find; knock, and it shall be opened unto you.

10 For every one that asketh receiveth; and he that seeketh findeth; and to him that knocketh it shall be opened.

11 If a son shall ask bread of any of you that is a father, will he give him a stone? or if he ask a fish, will he for a fish give him a serpent?

12 Or if he shall ask an egg, will he offer him a scorpion?

13 If ye then, being evil, know how to give good gifts unto your children: how much more shall your heavenly Father give the Holy Spirit to them that ask him?

Jesus indicates clearly that if we ask God to fill us with the Holy Spirit, God will not trick us and give us something evil. The Holy Spirit is not evil. Jesus warns us against calling the Holy Ghost an evil spirit (Mk. 3:28-30). In other words, we do not have to fear that we will receive something evil when we ask God to fill us with the Holy Spirit. God will indeed give us the Holy Spirit when we ask Him. Additionally, every individual who receives the baptism in the Holy Spirit also receives the ability to speak in tongues. Remember, God gives the ability to speak in other tongues, but the individual must do the speaking in other tongues. This is similar to the fact that God gives newborn babies the ability to use their vocal cords to make sounds with their mouth. God does not take control of the newborn and make sounds come out of his/her mouth. God gives the baby the ability, but the baby must choose to make sounds come out of his or her mouth.

In similar fashion, the same is true with believers that are baptized in the Holy Ghost. God gives the Spirit-filled believer the ability to speak in other tongues, but the believer must choose to speak the syllables or words out of his or her mouth, that the Spirit enables him or her to speak--otherwise nothing will be spoken. God will not take control of a believer's mouth and speak through it. It is God's desire that we all be saved, filled with the Holy Ghost, and speak with tongues. Are you ready?

Receive by Faith

Jesus says, "And these signs shall follow them that believe; In my name shall they cast out devils; they shall speak with new tongues" (Mk. 16:17). We have the authority to speak in tongues in Jesus' name. There is no authority on earth greater than the authority of Jesus.

Even if your denomination, church pastor, or Bible commentary teaches against speaking in tongues, their authority is not greater than the authority of Jesus! Jesus said, "All authority has been given to me in heaven and on earth," (Matt. 28:18b, New American Standard Bible).

Not only has Jesus given us his authority to speak in tongues, he has given us the power of attorney to use his name. He says, "In my name...they shall speak with new tongues" (Mk. 16:17). Therefore, if we can name a particular denomination that teaches against speaking in tongues; or if you can name a particular pastor that teaches against speaking in tongues; or if you can name a particular commentary that teaches against speaking in tongues, their name is not greater than the name of Jesus! Paul states:

Philippians 2:9-11
9 Wherefore God also hath highly exalted him, and given him a name which is above every name:

10 That at the name of Jesus every knee should bow, of things in heaven, and things in earth, and things under the earth;
11 And that every tongue should confess that Jesus is Lord, to the glory of God the Father.

Jesus authorized us to speak in tongues. He then confirms our authorization by giving us the legitimacy of his name. If God be for us, He is greater than the world that is against us. Therefore, let us receive the baptism of the Holy Spirit and start speaking in tongues.

I want to lead you in a prayer to receive the baptism of the Holy Spirit with the evidence of speaking in other tongues. Once you pray the prayer, open your mouth, and by faith begin to speak aloud whatever utterance, syllables, or words you can speak out. Do not wait for the presence or the absence of a certain feeling, before you start speaking in other tongues. Act by faith. All believers must receive the baptism in the Holy Ghost by faith, not by feelings.

You will not know what the words will sound like, until you by faith speak them out aloud. Remember, speaking in other tongues is speaking in a language that is unknown to you, so you will not have any idea how the words or syllables will sound. Remember, God will not take over your mouth and speak through you. Each individual must do his or her own speaking in tongues. The Holy Ghost only gives us the ability to speak in tongues. The Holy Ghost will not talk in tongues. **You** must do the talking in tongues.

After you pray the prayer, do not say a single word in English or in your common language: not even words like "Thank you Lord" or "Praise you Jesus." No one can speak in two languages at the same time. No one can speak Spanish and Italian at the same time. No one can speak in English and speak in tongues at the same time. Therefore, please refrain from speaking any words in English, or in your common language, but speak out of your mouth, only words or syllables in unknown tongues.

Following is a prayer that asks God to fill you with His Holy Spirit and give you the evidence of speaking in other tongues. First, simply read the prayer aloud, so that you will be aware of what you are asking God to do for you.

PRAYER:

Dear Heavenly Father, I come to You, confessing my faith in the Lord Jesus Christ and in Your Word. I accept Jesus as my Salvation and Lord. I am saved in Jesus' name. I desire now to be filled with the Holy Spirit and to speak in other tongues. I understand that You will not take control of my vocal cords and speak in tongues through me. I understand that it is You who gives me the ability to speak in other tongues, but it is I who must do the actual speaking in other tongues.

Right now, Lord, I ask You in Jesus' name to fill me with the Holy Ghost and give me the evidence of speaking in other tongues. Right now, by faith I receive the Holy Ghost in a greater measure into my life. Thank You, Lord, for filling me with the Holy Spirit, in Jesus' name. I open my mouth right now, and I begin to speak in other tongues. In Jesus' name. Amen.

If you desire for God to fill you with the Holy Ghost and give you the evidence of speaking in other tongues, in a moment pray the above prayer aloud to God. When you finish praying, open your mouth, and symbolically drink in the Holy Ghost by faith. Then begin to speak out of your mouth by faith, the words or syllables that you can speak forth out of your mouth. The words or syllables that you will speak out of your mouth will sound unfamiliar to you and may sound like gibberish ("stammering lips"). This is because you will be speaking in a foreign (unknown) tongue. Remember again, **you** must do the speaking in tongues. The Holy Spirit is not going to do the speaking for you. **You** must initiate the speaking by faith. Speaking in simple tongues is solely under your control. If **you** do not speak, nothing will be spoken. Pray the prayer now, and exercise your faith. Receive the Holy Ghost and begin to speak in tongues, in Jesus' name.

Praise God

Praise God for filling you with His Holy Spirit, and for giving you the evidence of speaking in other tongues. You are now in a noble line of brothers and sisters who are filled with the Holy Ghost and who speak in tongues: Jesus, the twelve Apostles, the Apostle Paul, Mary (the mother of Jesus), Jesus' brothers, and millions of other Christian believers.

Continue to speak, pray, praise, and worship God in your new prayer language every day. In addition, seek the fellowship of other Spirit-filled believers. They can encourage you more in your new walk with the Lord. The fellowship of other Spirit-filled believers can also help you continue to grow in the things of the Lord. Share this book with a friend, so that he or she can also receive these great gifts from God.

Remember:

Acts 2:39
39 For the promise is unto you, and to your children and to all that are afar off, even as many as the Lord our God shall call.

Hallelujah! Glory to God!

Endnotes

[1] Dan Cheatham, "Acts Chapter 2 – 30 AD – Day of Pentecost – 120," Pentecost & Tongues [Internet]. 2007 [cited 2012 Jan 8]; 1, Available from: http://devotionalnet.faithsite.com/uploads/147/76536.pdf.

[2] Kenneth E. Hagin, Welcome to God's Family: a Foundational Guide for Spirit-Filled Living, rev. ed. (Tulsa, Oklahoma: RHEMA Bible Church, aka Kenneth Hagin Ministries, Inc. 20001), 6.

[3] Kenneth E. Hagin, The Holy Spirit and the Gifts, (Tulsa, Oklahoma: RHEMA Bible Church, aka Kenneth Hagin Ministries, Inc. 1991), 134.

[4] James Strong, The Strong's Exhaustive Concordance of the Bible, (Nashville, Tennessee, Thomas Nelson Publishers, 1990), s.v. "dunamis,"

[5] Ibid., s.v. "dunamis,"

[6] James Strong, The New Strong's Exhaustive Concordance of the Bible, (Nashville, Tennessee, Thomas Nelson Publishers, 1990), s.v. "oikodomeo,"

[7] Kenneth E. Hagin, Welcome to God's Family" a Foundational Guide for Spirit-Filled Living, rev. ed. (USA, RHEMA Bible Church, aka Kenneth Hagin Ministries, Inc. 2001), 59.

[8] Noah Webster and others, Webster's New Universal Unabridged Dictionary, rev. ed. (New York: New World Dictionaries/Simon and Schuster, 1979), s.v. "battery,"

[9] James Strong, The Strong's Exhaustive Concordance of the Bible, (Nashville, Tennessee, Thomas Nelson Publishers, 1990), s.v. "embrimaomai,"

[10] Ibid., s.v. "stenagmos,"

[11] Ibid., s.v. "stenazo,"

[12] Webster's New Universal Unabridged Dictionary, rev. ed. (New York: Simon & Schuster, 1979) s.v. "intercession,"

[13] Ibid., s.v. "inaudible,"

[14] Ibid., s.v. "inaudible,"

[15] James Strong, The New Strong's Exhaustive Concordance of the Bible, (Nashville, Tennessee, Thomas Nelson Publishers, 1990), s.v. "alalletos,"

[16] F.F. Bruce, Tyndale New Testament Commentaries: Romans rev. ed. (Grand Rapids, Michigan: William B. Eerdmans Publishing Company, 1993), 165.

[17] James Strong, The New Strong's Exhaustive Concordance of the Bible, (Nashville, Tennessee, Thomas Nelson Publishers, 1990), s.v. "parakletos,"

[18] Kenneth S. Wuest, Word Studies in the Greek New Testament, vol. lll, (Grand Rapids, Michigan: Wm. B. Eerdmans Publishing Company, 1998), 90.

[19] Alfred Edersheim, The Life and Times of Jesus the Messiah: Complete and Unabridged in One Volume (United States of America: Hendrickson Publishers, Inc., 2002), 7.

[20] Brian Knowles, Hebrew Roots Feature: "Which Language Did Jesus Speak – Aramaic or Hebrew?," (Winter2012),http://www.godward.org/Hebrew20Rootsdid%20jesus%20speak%hebrew.htm.

[21] Kaari Ward and others, eds., Jesus and His Times (Pleasantville, New York: The Reader's Digest Association, Inc., 1987), 132.

[22] Ibid., 151.

[23] Alfred Edersheim, The Life and Times of Jesus the Messiah (Grand Rapids, Michigan: Wm. B. Eerdmans Publishing Company, 1971), 129.

[24] Ibid., 132.

[25] Alfred Edersheim, Sketches of Jewish Social Life (Peabody, Massachusetts: Hendrickson Publishers, Inc., 2003), 253.

[26] Alfred Edersheim, The Life and Times of Jesus the Messiah (Grand Rapids, Michigan: Wm. B. Eerdmans Publishing Company, 1971), 253.

[27] Alfred Edersheim, The Temple: Its Ministry and Services (Peabody, Massachusetts: Hendrickson Publishers, Inc., 2002), 23.

[28] Merrill C. Tenney and others, eds. The Zondervan Pictorial Encyclopedia of the Bible, vol. 2, (Grand Rapids, Michigan: Zondervan, 1976), 58.

[29] Kenneth E. Hagin, The Holy Spirit and His Gifts (RHEMA Bible Church, AKA Kenneth Hagin Ministries, Inc., 1991), 149.

[30] Ibid., 157.

[31] Ibid., 157.

[32] Merriam Webster's Collegiate Dictionary, rev. ed. (Springfield, Mass.: Merriam-Webster, Incorporated, 1997), s.v. "interpret".

[33] Kenneth E. Hagin, The Holy Spirit and His Gifts (RHEMA Bible Church, AKA Kenneth Hagin Ministries, Inc., 1991), 149.

[34] Alexander Balmain Bruce and Marcus Dods, The Expositor's Greek Testament, vol.1, (United States of America: Hendrickson Publishers, Inc., 2002), 331.

[35] Alfred Edersheim, The Life and Times of Jesus the Messiah (Grand Rapids, Michigan: Wm. B. Eerdmans Publishing Company, 1971), 130.

Printed in the United States
by Baker & Taylor Publisher Services